TIBET
TRANSHIMALAYA

In the same series:

ANATOLIA I (From the beginnings to the end of the 2nd millennium B.C.)	U. Bahadır Alkım, Professor at the University of Istanbul
ANATOLIA II (From the 1st millennium B.C. to the end of the Roman period)	Henri Metzger, Professor at the University of Lyons
BYZANTIUM	Antoine Bon, Professor at the University of Lyons
CELTS AND GALLO-ROMANS	Jean Jacques-Hatt, Professor at the University of Strasbourg
CENTRAL AMERICA	Claude F. Baudez, Research Professor at the Centre National de la Recherche Scientifique (C.N.R.S.), Paris
CENTRAL ASIA	Aleksandr Belenitsky, Professor at the Archaeological Institute of Leningrad
CHINA	Vadime Elisseeff, Curator at the Cernuschi Museum, Paris
CRETE	Nicolas Platon, former Superintendent of Antiquities, Crete; former Director of the Acropolis Museum, Athens
CYPRUS	Vassos Karageorghis, Director of the Archaeological Museum, Nicosia
EGYPT	Jean Leclant, Professor at the Sorbonne, Paris
THE ETRUSCANS	Raymond Bloch, Professor at the Sorbonne, Paris
THE GERMANIC PEOPLES	Rolf Hachmann, Professor at the University of Saarbrücken
GREAT MORAVIA	Anton Točik, Director of the Archaeological Institute of Nitra (Czechoslovakia)
GREECE I (Mycenaean and geometric periods)	Nicolas Platon, former Superintendent of Antiquities, Crete; former Director of the Acropolis Museum, Athens
GREECE II (Post-geometric periods)	Jean Marcadé, Professor at the University of Bordeaux
INDIA	Maurizio Taddei, Inspector of Oriental Art and Archaeology, Rome
INDOCHINA	Bernard P. Groslier, Curator of Historical Monuments, Angkor; Director of Archaeological Research, Ecole Française d'Extrême-Orient
INDONESIA	Bernard P. Groslier, Curator of Historical Monuments, Angkor; Director of Archaeological Research, Ecole Française d'Extrême-Orient

JAPAN	Vadime Elisseeff, Curator at the Cernuschi Museum, Paris
MESOPOTAMIA	Jean-Claude Margueron, Member of the French Institute of Archaeology, Beirut
MEXICO	Jacques Soustelle
PERSIA I (From the origins to the Achaemenids)	Jean-Louis Huot, Member of the French Institute of Archaeology, Beirut
PERSIA II (From the Seleucids to the Sassanids)	Vladimir G. Lukonin, Head of the Oriental Department, Hermitage Museum, Leningrad
PERU	† Rafael Larco Hoyle, Director of the Rafael Larco Herrera Museum, Lima
PREHISTORY	Denise de Sonneville-Bordes, Ph. D.
ROMANIA	Constantin Daicoviciu, Director of the Archaeological Institute of Cluj, and Emil Condurachi, Director of the Archaeological Institute of Bucharest
ROME	Gilbert Picard, Professor at the Sorbonne, Paris
SOUTHERN CAUCASUS	Boris B. Piotrovsky, Director of the Hermitage Museum, Leningrad
SOUTHERN SIBERIA	Mikhail Gryaznov, Professor at the Archaeological Institute, Leningrad
SYRIA-PALESTINE I (Ancient Orient)	Jean Perrot, Head of the French Archaeological Mission in Israel
SYRIA-PALESTINE II (Classical Orient)	Michael Avi Yonah, Professor at the University of Jerusalem, and David Ussishkin of the University of Jerusalem
THAILAND	M. C. Sudhadradis Diskul, Professor at the Silpakorn University, Bangkok
URARTU	Boris B. Piotrovsky, Director of the Hermitage Museum, Leningrad

ARCHAEOLOGIA MVNDI

Series prepared under the direction of
Jean Marcadé, Professor of Archaeology
at the University of Bordeaux

GIUSEPPE TUCCI

TRANSHIMALAYA

Translated from the French by James Hogarth
33 illustrations in colour, 177 in black and white

NAGEL PUBLISHERS, GENEVA . PARIS . MUNICH

ISBN 2-8263-0575-1

© 1973 by NAGEL PUBLISHERS, GENEVA (SWITZERLAND)
All rights reserved in all countries, including the U.S.S.R.
Printed in Switzerland

CONTENTS

Preface 9
Note on Pronunciation 11
Introduction 13
Chapter I: The Prehistoric and Protohistorical Periods 33

                The Material: Small Finds 33
                Caves 40
                Megaliths, Tombs and Shrines 50

Chapter II: The Historical Period 61

                The Royal Tombs 61
                Civil and Military Architecture 64
                Temples 77
                Chötens 96

Chapter III: The Genesis of Tibetan Art 137

                The Influence of Neighbouring Countries 137
                Foreign Works and Local Imitations 178
                The Kashmiri and Nepalese Styles 141
                Towards a Tibetan *Koine* 184
                Stone Sculpture 195

Conclusion 199
Notes 201
Comparative Chronology 207
Bibliography 211
List of Illustrations 219
Index 235

PREFACE

*T**he reader may be puzzled to find, in a series devoted to studying the diverse aspects of archaeological research in the various provinces of its vast empire, a volume concerned with the Transhimalayan region — i.e. broadly the central and western parts of the autonomous region of Tibet in the Chinese People's Republic. And indeed, since Chinese scholars are just beginning to take an interest in Tibetan archaeology, this volume cannot seek, like other volumes in the series, to review the problems, the methods and the results of a scientifically conducted exploration of the country's past. The aim must therefore be the more modest one of drawing up a provisional inventory of the visible remains and the works of art which have survived the centuries, setting out a preliminary basis for discussion, and outlining a programme of work for the future.*

The interest and novelty of the present study are therefore evident. Professor Tucci is undoubtedly the greatest living expert in his field and has himself discovered, during his travels in Tibet, much of the material at present available. Most of his published works are not readily accessible to the general reader, and he has therefore undertaken to summarise in this volume the results of his work and his main conclusions. For a scholar the writing of a book of this kind is not without its hazards; but Professor Tucci's readers will appreciate the privilege and the opportunity now offered to them.

J.M.

The material published in this work is the harvest of over thirty years of study and research, and some of the illustrations, obtained in difficult conditions over a long period of years, may not be up to the highest standards of quality. But since most of the photographs are now the only evidence we have on remains which have since been destroyed or are otherwise inaccessible the publishers have thought it right to make them available to the general public just as they are, since any retouching would prejudice their authenticity. They are confident that the readers of this book will agree with this decision.

We should like to express our sincere gratitude to Professor Tucci for allowing us to publish this quite unique documentation and for his illuminating discussion of the material he presents.

NOTE ON PRONUNCIATION

The letter *š* is pronounced like English *sh*; *ž* like the *s* in "leisure". The soft occlusives *(g, j, d, b, dz)* at the beginning of a word or syllable are pronounced hard *(k, c, t, p, ts)* but in a lower tone.

The letters *g, d, b, m* and *a* used as prefixes or following *r, l* and *s* are not pronounced (exception: *lha*, pronounced *lha*), but preserve the original value of the soft sounds: e.g. *gaṅ*, pronounced *kang*, but *sgaṅ*, pronounced *gang*.

Y, r and *l* after initial consonants cause some sound changes. *Pya, phya* and *bya* are pronounced as palatals, like English *cha* and *ja*; *mya* like *ña (nya)*. *Kra, tra* and *pra* are all pronounced as a cerebral *ṭa*; similarly *k'ra* and *p'ra* are pronounced *ṭha; gra, dra* and *bra* are pronounced *ṭa;* and *sra* is pronounced *sa*.

A consonant followed by *l* disappears: e.g. *bla-ma* is pronounced *lama* and *rluṅ lung*. Exception: *zla* is pronounced *da*.

As finals *d, l* and *s* are silent, but produce a softening of the vowel: e.g. *brgyad, rgol* and *lus* are pronounced *gyä, gö* and *lü*. *N* also produces a softening but is still heard: e.g. *brtsan*, pronounced *tsän (or tsen)*.

INTRODUCTION

Definition of the Enquiry[1]

The travellers, relatively few in number, who have found their way to Tibet have almost always been concerned to describe the customs of the country or have been mainly interested in geographical, sociological or religious research. Even those who have studied the cultural history of Tibet have mostly neglected the archaeological aspects of their subject and devoted their attention to questions of more strictly religious or liturgical interest. In my own travels in Tibet I concentrated on its archaeology and the history of its art, publishing the results of my work in the seven volumes of *Indo-Tibetica*[2], which is principally concerned with western Tibet, and in a substantial work, *Tibetan Painted Scrolls*[3], which as its title indicates deals with the painted cotton or silk scrolls displayed in temples or carried by travellers as talismans. I was also able during my travels, and particularly in the monasteries to which I enjoyed access, to collect much other material which made it possible to suggest comparisons with artistic trends in other countries which played their part in creating the particular art forms and artistic schools of Tibet. The task was not always an easy one, for the statues and paintings of which the temples were full were heaped together in confusion, and frequently the statues were disfigured by the gilt varnish applied to the faces each year for liturgical reasons. Moreover the monks would not always allow photographs to be taken inside the temples, and it was never possible to use magnesium lighting. Later, in 1948, I visited the tombs of the Tibetan kings — in very bad weather conditions — and the most ancient remains in central Tibet. I was able in this way to gather a very considerable amount of material, but this is mostly of documentary rather than artistic value, since as a result of the conditions in which the photographs were taken (some of them by Indian photographers when my own assistants were not allowed to accompany me) they are not all up to the highest standards of quality. I was, however, able to acquire a number of objects which could be photographed in Italy with rather more care. I must add that in making a selection from this material the chronological limits set by the series of which this volume forms part have sometimes imposed a constraint.

It must be made clear at the outset that Tibetan archaeology, if by archaeology we mean the results of properly conducted excavation, is still in a state of limbo. Even since Tibet was integrated into the Chinese People's Republic there has not been, so far as I am aware, any archaeological excavation in any part of Tibet; nor have I seen a single reference to any such research in any of the Chinese journals cited in the Bibliography, although Chinese scholars have now started publishing preliminary articles on the art treasures preserved in the oldest monasteries of Tibet. For the moment, therefore, we can do no more than outline a programme of possible future archaeological research, drawing attention to the problems to be solved and noting the sites and areas of most interest from the point of view of archaeology or art history. Apart from this there are two immediate tasks to be undertaken. The first is to draw up an inventory, based on the surviving material and any available historical sources, of the works of art brought into Tibet from other areas and, if possible, to establish when they were brought in. The second is to determine what influence these works of art, and artists coming into Tibet from other areas, had on the development of the specific characteristics which gave Tibetan art — whether painting or sculpture — its distinctive individuality.

I have referred to foreign influences on Tibet, for these are attested by much surviving material; and the Tibetans themselves are well aware of these influences and have preserved the memory of them. We cannot therefore ignore these facts in this first outline of Tibetan archaeology and its programme of future research: we must indeed depend exclusively on them. This makes it necessary to extend in some degree the accepted meaning of the term "archaeology", which for our purposes must be taken as including not only the collection of material and the use of such limited archaeological data as we possess but also a study of the wider field of art history and, more specifically, the circumstances in which Tibetan art came into being. Anticipating later discussion for the sake of clarity, we may note that our survey can be brought to a close about the end of the Sakyapa *(Sa skya pa)* period, or perhaps rather later (13th to 15th centuries), when a variety of artistic trends were blended to give Tibetan art its distinctive character, so that it represents the expression of a particular sensibility. This did not of course prevent other influences from making themselves felt at a later stage in areas or in individual monasteries which had particular contacts with other countries.

But although our survey of Tibetan archaeology, in the narrow sense of the term, must seek merely to draw up a programme for the future, our examination of the genesis of Tibetan modes of artistic expression is not similarly restricted. Architecture for the most part followed its own traditional patterns, but art was exposed to many influences from outside Tibet. In addition to its relations with Kashmir, Central Asia and Bengal, Tibet always maintained close contacts with Nepal. The influence of China was felt as early as the period of the kings in Tibet (7th to 9th centuries) and again in the Sakyapa period (13th century), in the time of the Mongol (Yüan) dynasty. This influence was exerted particularly in painting, and can always be felt, particularly in eastern Tibet and in certain iconographic types like the Lokapālas and the Arhats. At Phüntshokling *(P'un ts'ogs gliṅ)* we find styles of painting of Indian origin practised until the 16th century, and there are references to Indian artists as late as the time of the fifth Dalai Lama (1617–1682).

2

3

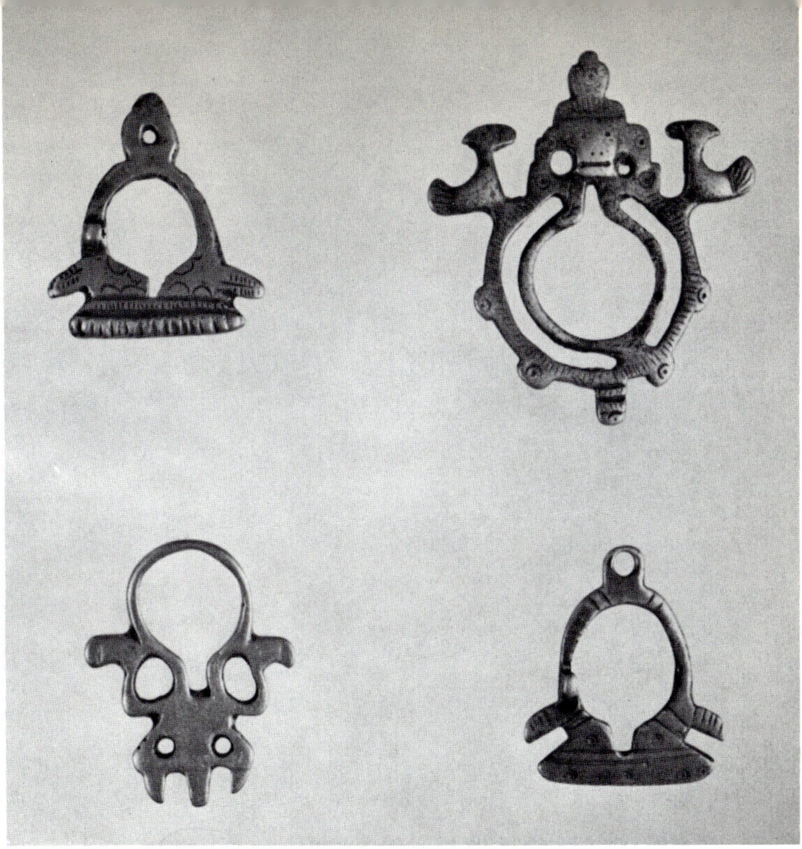

4

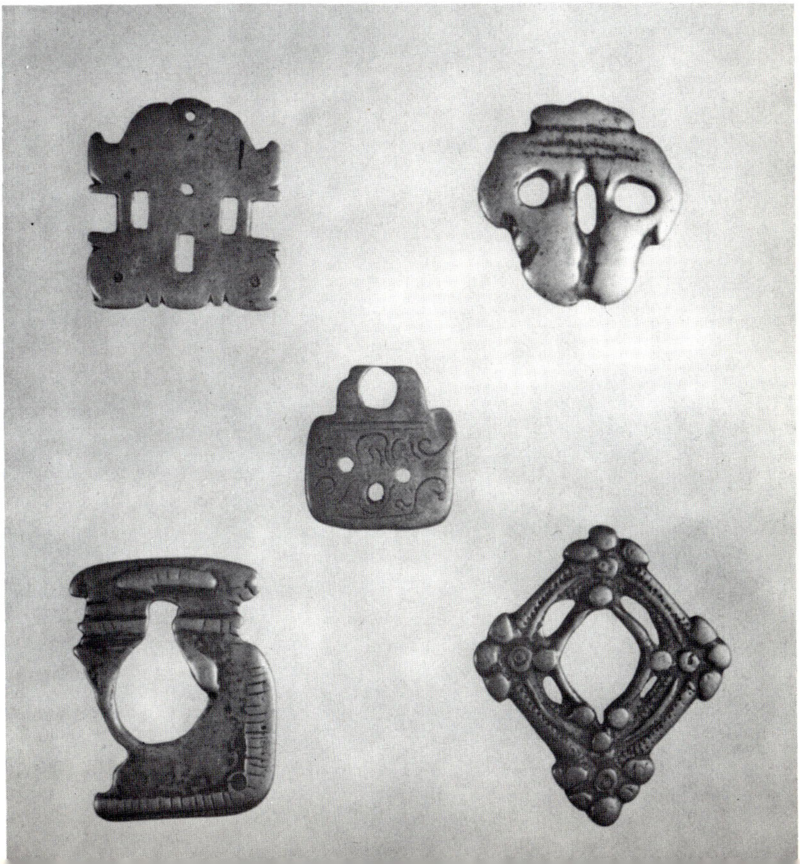

5

6

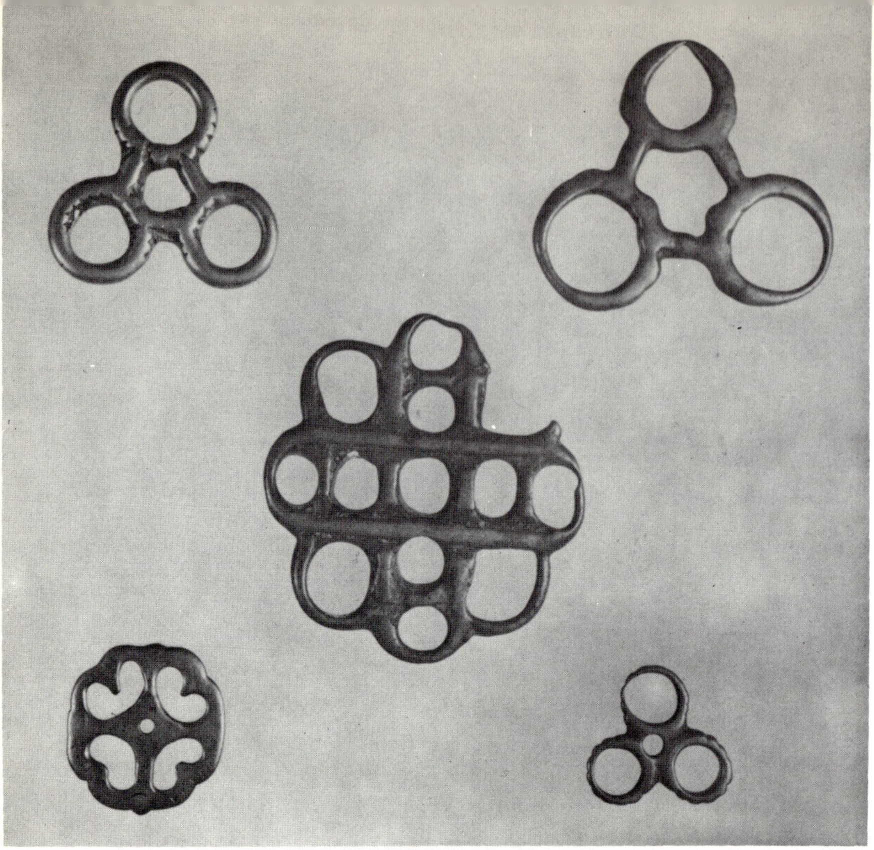

7

8

9

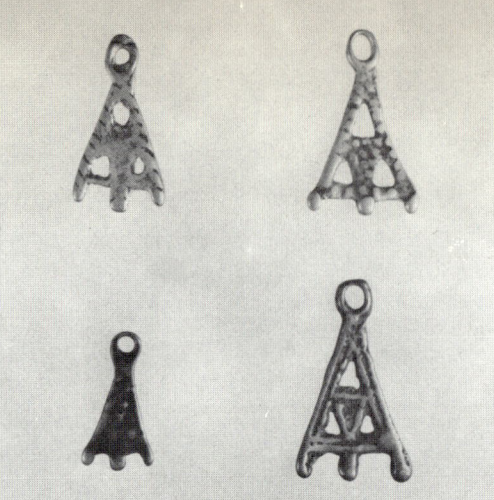

10

11

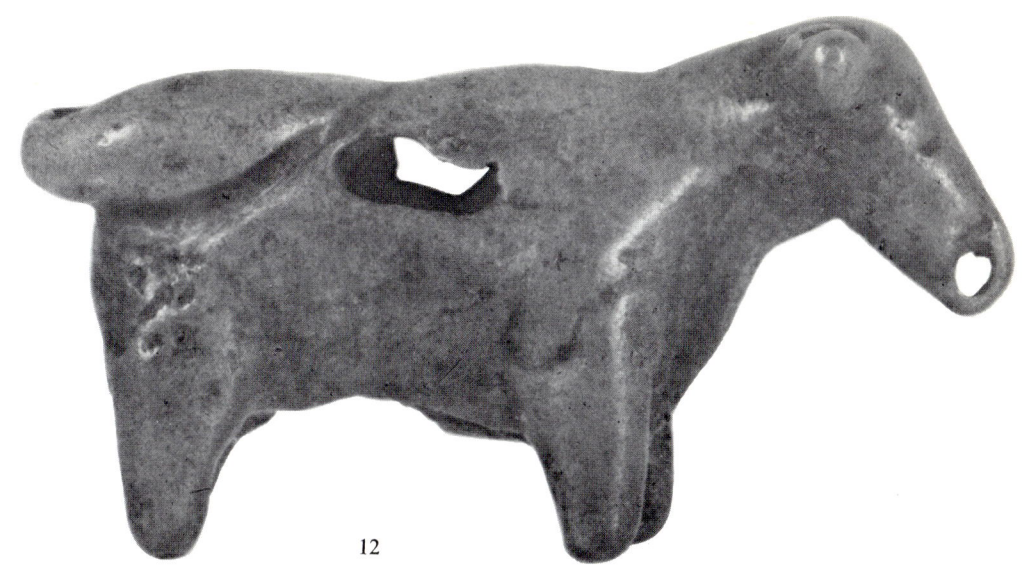

12

13

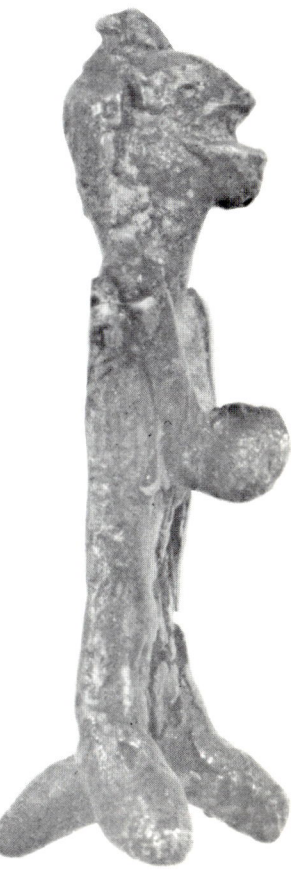

14

15

16

17 18

19 20

21

22

24

23

25

28

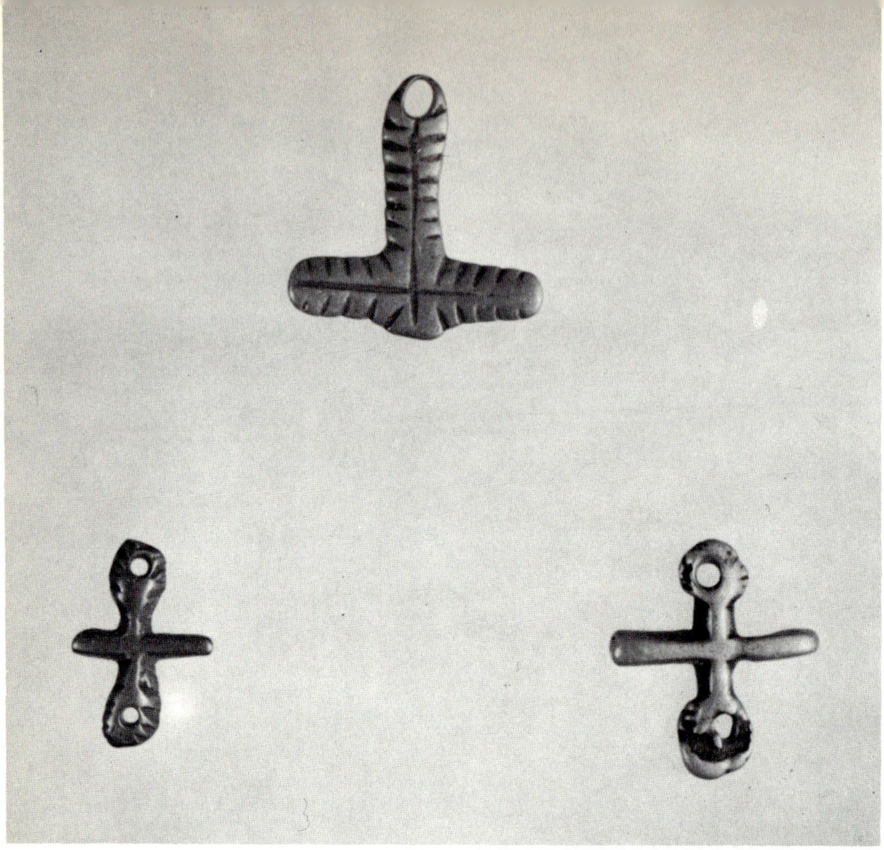

29

30

31

32

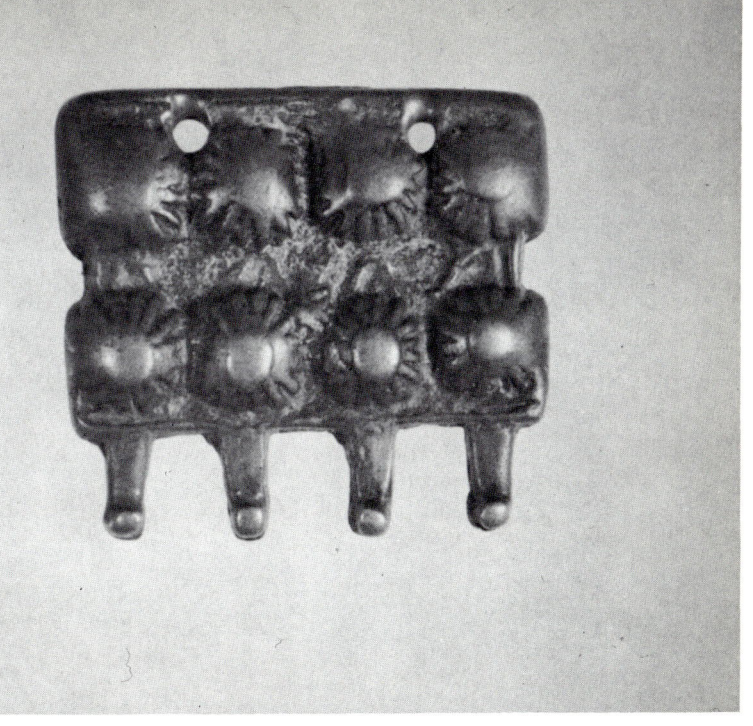

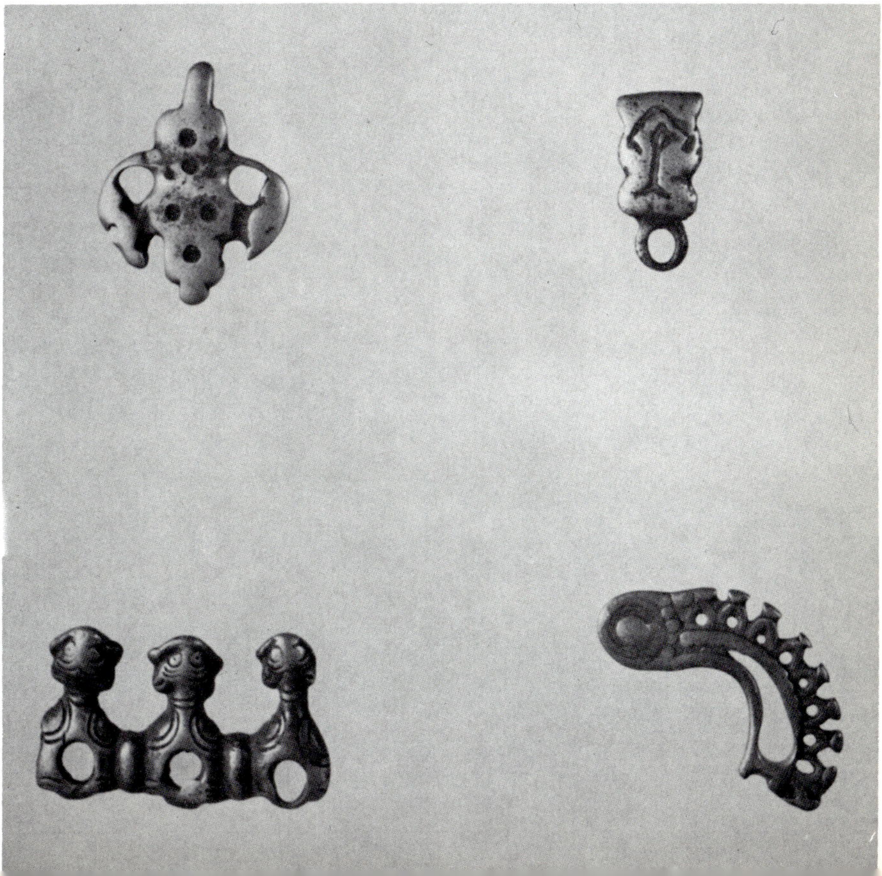

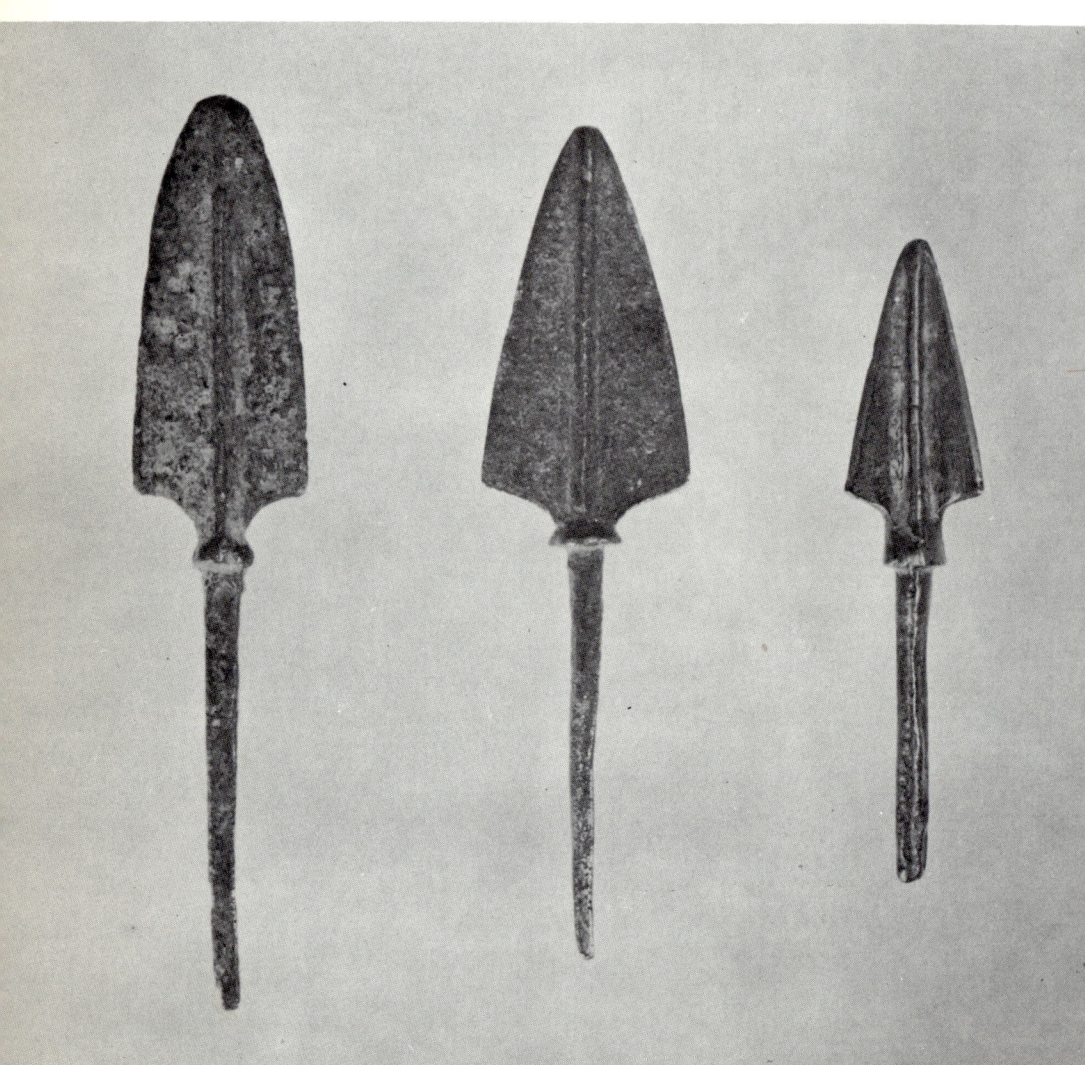

THE PREHISTORIC AND PROTOHISTORICAL PERIODS

I

The Material: Small Finds

The archaeology of Tibet is thus based essentially on objects found by chance or on those remains which have survived. Given the religious atmosphere of the country, it would have been impossible before the integration of Tibet into the Chinese People's Republic to carry out excavations of any kind, particularly on those sites which are traditionally regarded as most significant for the history and culture of Tibet. As we shall see, there are numerous caves which we know with certainty were inhabited in prehistoric times; but when I sought to explore one such cave at Luk in western Tibet I was obliged to abandon the excavation, the hostility of the village people being all too evident.

A recent article by Mrs Tai Erh-chien[4] refers to the discovery of a skeleton near Nyelam *(Ñe lam)*, between Nepal and Tibet — not excavated in a tomb but discovered by chance buried in a river bed. Stone implements of the Neolithic period were also found.

For the moment, therefore, in the absence of exact points of reference and objects which can be dated with certainty — a situation about which there will be more to say later — any division into a prehistoric and a protohistorical period must necessarily be very uncertain. The boundary between the two periods is to some extent arbitrary, for the real history of Tibet begins in the 7th century with the earliest information afforded by the Chinese sources, followed at a later date by the first documents which can properly be called Tibetan. Until systematic excavations have been carried out, however, we shall be unable to determine with certainty whether all the objects to be discussed in this chapter date from the pre-Buddhist period: some of them, indeed, do undoubtedly date from Buddhist times and thus fall within the historical period. All that can be said, therefore, is that although the dating of these objects is speculative and uncertain they do nevertheless form a distinctive group which in general bears no relationship to the arts and crafts of Tibet as we know them from material which can be dated with certainty and is fully in line with articles of known function which are familiar to us in the historical period.

Objects of this kind are found by peasants working in the fields: I am thinking in particular of the objects known in Tibet as *thokde* (*t'og rdeu*, "stone fallen from the sky") or *thoding* (*mt'o ldiṅ*, "high-flying"): i.e. "thunder stones". The name might suggest lithic material found by chance, like arrowheads or axes; but in fact I have never seen any examples of this kind.

In the course of my travels in Tibet I have come across a fair number of these objects, but have only very seldom been able to buy one, for the Tibetans consider them as potent talismans and are reluctant to part with them. This is particularly so if they are fortunate enough to collect nine of them — nine being a sacred number to the Bonpo, adepts of the old Tibetan religion which has left many traces in the religious beliefs of the people.

Taken as a whole, these objects show close links with the art of the Central Asian steppes and bear witness to relationships, either direct or indirect, with other centres of culture, as Professor Bussagli and I have indicated (Tucci, 1935; Bussagli, 1949). More recently (1961) Goldman has carried out further work in this field and has suggested connections with Iran. Links of this kind are indeed probable, for there were undoubtedly contacts between Tibet (particularly western Tibet) and the Iranian cultures at a very early date, and it is likely that artistic and decorative themes would pass from Iran to Tibet as a result of migration and trade.

Goldman's hypothesis is, however, valid only for some of the objects published by Professor Bussagli and myself; for we must not overlook the other element which — influenced though it may have been by Iranian culture — is strongly represented in Tibet and is still used in the decoration of various objects: the art of the steppes, which still survives after many centuries, particularly in northern and north-eastern Tibet. We must not, therefore, forget the migrations of the Yüeh-chi in these regions.

The skill of Tibetan craftsmen in forging metal is recorded in the early Chinese sources[5]. We do not know what metals were worked in this period, but they certainly included copper, bronze and iron, the working of which may have been brought in by different routes. It is not possible to determine on the basis of archaeological evidence when iron-working — a craft which no doubt conferred a magical prestige on its practitioners — first began; but I regard as questionable the view expressed by W. Ruben[6] and after him by S. Hummel[7], following up suggestions by Heine-Geldern[8], that the art of iron-working was introduced in the course of a migration from the Pontic region.

It is difficult to establish the use or the significance of the objects in question. Some have a purely functional character — buckles, buttons, small bells and pendants *(Plates 2, 22–24, 26, 30)* — and this in itself makes their dating still more uncertain[9]. It is clear, however, that some of them are of a sacred character: this is the case, I believe, with those which have a circle as their predominant motif *(Plate 16:* a turquoise in the centre, with nine hemispherical "drops" round it), either in what can provisionally be described as a pendant or in the form of a number of associated circles, usually three *(Plates 3, 4, 5, below, and 6)*. Often the circle is not closed but is open-ended[10]. The central theme, representing the centre of the world and thus of the tent or the house, conceived in the image of the universe, is too familiar to require further discussion. More complex, however, is the significance of the motifs at the ends of the open-ended circle. These had some particular meaning, as is shown by the occurrence of figures of animals, either represented naturally *(Plates 3, 4, above)* or so highly stylised as to retain only a distant resemblance to the original *(Plate 4, below)*, as well as by comparison with some rather similar examples found in Iran *(Plates 7, right, and 8)*. Significant also in this respect are the figures of birds (but not the *k'yuṅ*) either facing one another or turned towards what may be a mountain *(Plate 4, above, right, between two animals)*[11].

I am also inclined to attribute a sacred character to the central figure in *Plate 6*, with its thirteen circles; for thirteen was a sacred number in the Bonpo religion, as in others. Similarly we cannot attribute a purely functional significance to the triangles shown in *Plate 10*. They were undoubtedly intended to be hung from something, as is shown by the eyelet through which a cord could be passed; but these triangles, which all end in a "drop" and, with one exception, all have three empty spaces within them, cannot in my view have been purely decorative in intention. They are too small to have formed part of the trappings of a horse, and are evidently pieces of personal jewellery which may have been used as talismans, based on religious conceptions of whose significance we are ignorant.

It is easier to discuss the bronzes reproduced in *Plate 11*. Four of them undoubtedly represent the *khyung (k'yuṅ)*, which in Bonpo tradition was a sacred animal, contrasted with the demoniac *khading (mk'a' ldiṅ)*[12]. The *khyung* survived the decline of the Bonpo religion and found a place in popular tradition, becoming amalgamated with the Indian Garuḍa.

There are certain other objects which we must also regard as talismans, or religious symbols, or totemic or clan emblems: for example the representations *(Plates 19–21)* of four birds' heads set on the same body. It is difficult to define them more closely, for they have no resemblance either to eagles or to vultures: indeed to judge by their crests they may well be cocks, known in

Tibetan as *chapo (bya po)*. The four figures are divided into two groups of two, and as the eyelet at the top indicates they were intended to be hung round someone's neck or on a horse's harness.

It is difficult to identify the creature represented in *Plate 12*. Probably it is a bear (either *dom*, the brown bear, or *dred*, the tawny bear, an animal which figures in Tibetan folklore). *Plate 13* represents the handle or terminal ornament of some instrument in the form of a highly stylised ram, while in *Plate 25 (left)* it is easy to recognise two animals rearing up on their hind legs and facing one another, a motif of common occurrence in the art of Asia, from Mesopotamia to Siberia.

The only representation of the human figure is the one on the thin strip of bronze reproduced in *Plate 14*. In this figure the two hands are shown palms upwards, held against the breast and apparently supporting some objects which can no longer be distinguished. The features are crudely depicted, and the figure appears to be wearing a hat with the top bent backwards. It may represent an offering-bearer, or perhaps a god. It seems to me to show resemblances to certain similar objects recently discovered in eastern Iran.

Plate 24 clearly shows a buckle with a crude representation of an animal's head in the centre. Of great interest, too, is the bronze representation *(Plate 28)* of an animal — a feline, perhaps a lion — treated in similar fashion to an example from Inner Mongolia[13].

These objects come from various parts of western Tibet, Tsang *(gTsaṅ)* and central Tibet. The find-spots, however, are of no particular significance, since in virtue of the apotropaic powers with which they were credited they may have been bought by nomads, and it is thus not possible to establish any clear connection between the places where they were acquired and the places where they were found. They can, therefore, only be classed together as the earliest evidence of Tibetan craftsmanship, produced within an ill-defined chronological period which may cover a range of several centuries, extending even into the Buddhist period.

Plate 1 is particularly important as an illustration of the spatio-temporal quality represented by the circle which is the image of the sky. It shows an open-ended circle surrounded by twelve animals, and although the object is worn and the decoration rather crudely executed there can be no doubt that this represents the animals of the duodecimal cycle — a rat, an ox, a tiger, a hare, a dragon, a snake, a horse, a monkey, a bird, a dog and a pig. The duodecimal cycle is used for dating purposes as early as the chronicles of Tun huang. The Bonpo gods known as Ghikö *(Gi k'od* or *Ge k'od)* were also closely associated with the annual cycle, since there were 360 of them[14]. The object illustrated, however, belongs to a later period, since it shows some degree of fusion with Buddhist beliefs, as exemplified by the eight auspicious signs depicted in the upper part of the object, the *ṭashitagye (bkra šis rtags brgyad)* — the umbrella, the goldfish, the jar containing treasure, the lotus, the shell, the knot, the standard, the wheel. It is thus evident that this object represents a mingling of older beliefs with the symbolism introduced by Buddhism.

To these examples can be added an iron corn-measure, inlaid with gold and silver, which is dated to the Yüan period *(Plate 112)*. The decoration, in which a cross can be clearly distinguished, shows affinities with similar examples studied by Hambis[15]. I refer to it here in order to show the continuity of the influences of foreign cultures.

The figure of a *Bos indicus* reproduced in *Plate 67* may have been imported from India, for the sacred animal of Tibet was not the ox — considered in India as the bearer of Śiva — but the white yak, which played a major rôle in Tibetan cosmology.

Plate 22 shows a concave bulla which may have served to contain a formula or a talisman. It can be seen as a kind of prototype of the *gau* of a later period — the small bronze or silver box in which sacred formulae were kept.

Some objects are clearly buttons of very similar type to those published by Rudenko[16], like a number of other items which are identical to material published by the same author[17].

There are also figures of monkeys *(Plates 17, 18)*. This theme is represented over a wide area, and has been found as far away as Minusinsk, where the monkey does not occur in the wild state; and it is hardly surprising to find it in Tibet, since according to tradition the Tibetan people arose from the union of a monkey — in which Buddhist thought saw an incarnation of Chenresik *(sPyan ras gzigs)* — with a female demon.

The two pendants shown in *Plate 29 (below)* belong to a later period. It seems reasonable to identify them as Nestorian crosses, like the one on the corn-measure already referred to, since we have a reference to a Nestorian bishop of Tibet[18], and many cross-like objects discovered in the Ordos region and elsewhere in China[19] can be attributed to the Nestorians (in some cases with an element of doubt). *Plate 11 (below, left)* very probably represents a dove, also a Nestorian symbol. There is nothing unlikely about the presence of Nestorians in Tibet in the time of the Yüan dynasty, since in this period there were many Nestorians in China and among the Mongols.

Another type of object found by peasants working in the fields consists of beads from necklaces, cylindrical in shape with tapered ends, made of a whitish fabric and decorated with brown lines or small brown circles. There is usually an odd number of circles. which gives the beads special value and significance. I have never managed to acquire any examples of these beads, since they command very high prices, being regarded as talismans of particular magical and protective power. Some of these objects, I was told, had been found in tombs.

These beads are known as *zigs*, and the small circles on them are called *mig* ("eyes"). They come from necklaces of a type which is very common in Asia, from the Near East to Iran and Central Asia. No positive conclusions can therefore be drawn from these finds: they merely prove, once again, that the peoples who lived in Tibet had contacts and trading exchanges with neighbouring countries from a very early period.

Other beads, made of glass paste, are similar to examples published by G.G. Seligman and H.C. Beck[20].

Also of very common occurrence all over Tibet are arrows with a central rib. The specimens in my own collection are made of iron, and are of a type which is so common that it is not possible to suggest even an approximate date *(Plate 33)*.

Caves

Caves, sometimes occurring in isolation and sometimes in groups, are very numerous in Tibet. In addition to the Luk caves already mentioned, still not completely explored, there are caves in the Nubra area and in Kun Lun[21] with wall decorations which appear to date from the 2nd millennium B.C.[22]. There are also caves at Lhatse *(Lha rtse) (Plate 34)*. Other caves near Yandogtsho *(Yar ạbrog mts'o) (Plate 36)*, which were apparently inhabited in prehistoric times, were briefly described by L.A.Waddell[23] in 1905; and there are others at Janthang *(Byaṅ t'aṅ?) (Plate 35)*, Yarlung *(Yar kluṅs) (Plate 37)* and Doṭakdsong *(rDo brag rdsoṅ)*. In western Tibet, at Tsaparang, Chang *(P'yaṅ or P'yi dbaṅ gdaṅ mk'ar?)*, Khyunglung *(K'yuṅ luṅ)*[24]

34, 35

36, 37

38, 39

40, 41

༄༅། །དུག་ཀང་ཁབ་སོ་སྩལ་པའི་གནས་
དང་འགོག་ན་ཡིག་ཚང་དུ་གསལ་
བྱི་ཤན་གྱི་ཕྱག་རྒྱས་བཏབ་ནས་
རྒྱལ་བྱི་ཚིགས་ནན་ཏར་བཟེ་
ནས་ལ་འབྲི་གཏན་མན་མཆིས་
པར་བྱི་ཤོ་ཡི་བྱུར་སྟུ་ད་
ད་ཕྱལ་ད་ལ་སའི་བྱི་རེ་ལྷ་བྲི་
བསྩུབ་བ་བཙན་གྱི་སོ་ད་བྱི་
ཕ་ག་ད་བར་བས་ལེ་ལེ་ཞིང་ཡང་
བཙོན་རི་ཡ་བསྲུས་ཀྱིས་འདི་
བའི་ནོ་ད་ནས་ཙོ་ན་ཀ་ས་
མན་ཤན་ན་རྒྱུར་བ་ད་བ་རྒྱ་
ཀྱི་བ་ཀྱི་ཕྱི་བ་སྐུར་བར་འཇིག་
རྟེན་ལས་། འདའ་འགས་མཛད་ད་
འཇིག་རྟེན་ཀྱི་ནུར་བ་གྱུར་ཡིན་
བ་ཡ་ཐམས་ཅད་རྒྱུར་བ་ད་བསྩུ་
འདིར་ལ་ཞེ་བ་ཙོ་ན་ཡ་བསྲུས་
རྗེ་བློན་ཀུན་ཀྱིས་དགུར་བ་ཕྱི་
བ་ར་བྱོ་ག་ཅིག་ཀ་ས་ཀྱི་ཡི་དྲ་
བར་བྱོ་ག་ཅིག་ཀ་ས་ཀྱི་ཡི་དྲ་

44

45

46

and elsewhere, there are numerous troglodytic settlements, with remains of castles and temples above ground. Other troglodytic centres are found at Lo (*Blo*, Mustang), north of Tukcha — i.e. in the part of Nepal, formerly independent or associated with Tibet, where the Tibetan language is still spoken. The Tibetan hermits were accustomed to spend much of their lives meditating in caves; and the Lepchas of Sikkim believe that men come down from the summits of the mountains into a cave and then return to the mountains after their death[25].

Milarepa, one of the most celebrated mystics of Tibet, spent most of his life in caves; the names of some of them are recorded by his biographers. Yerpa *(Yer pa)*, to the east of Lhasa[26], is a monastic settlement occupying a group of caves. The monastery of Rechungphuk *(Ras c'uṅ p'ug)* at Yarlung is built near a cave to which a famous ascetic, a disciple of Milarepa, retired to meditate.

Another very remarkable site, which has undoubtedly been regarded as sacred since very early times, is Pretapuri (also known as Tīrthapuri to the Indians, who go in pilgrimage to Mount Kailāsa), the city of the *Preta* (lemurs), where are numerous caves[27]. Other examples are a temple hewn from the rock in which Gayādhara once lived, the cave in which Sachen *(Sa c'en)* meditated at Sakya *(Sa skya)*, below the Labrangshar *(Bla braṅ šar)*, and the temple of Tshogyeltagmar *(mTs'o rgyal Brag dmar)*, which is attributed to Ṭhisongdetsen *(K'ri sroṅ lde brtsan)*.

We cannot of course be sure that all these caves, particularly those with troglodytic settlements, date from the prehistoric period. In some cases, as at Tsaparang, Chang and Khyunglung, the caves were probably used as dwellings only in winter, since in summer the whole population would move to the high plateaux with their flocks and herds, returning to the caves only when the cold weather came on. The situation may have been different in the caves at Lo (*Blo*, Mustang) and some of those occupied by hermits who were accustomed to spend much of their life, if not the whole of it, in caves. The problem can be solved only by archaeological investigation, as it has been solved, for example, in Swat, where a cave still occasionally occupied on wet and windy nights by the Gujars (who make annual seasonal migrations) has been carefully excavated, yielding important stratigraphic evidence which extends downwards from a top stratum of 16th–17th century Islamic pottery to the Upper Palaeolithic[28]. It does not seem probable that the caves occupied by hermits were invariably hewn from the rock by the hermits themselves: no doubt when they found one ready made they would be glad to take it over as their place of retreat. It must be the task of Chinese archaeologists to identify the caves which were already in existence in historical times, and then to determine by scientific excavation which of them reveal traces of early settlement and how far back that occupation goes.

It is possible, too, that some of these caves, particularly those situated near major settlements or royal residences, may have served as prisons in which offenders might be confined for many years[29].

Megaliths, Tombs and Shrines

On many sites in Tibet we find large stones set in the ground, either by themselves or in groups, arranged in circles or sometimes in square formations or in alignments. In the middle of the group there may be either one or three taller stones set erect like pilasters, left in their natural state without any dressing. When there are three of these standing stones the one in the middle is higher than the other two: we see this, for example, at Pu *(sPu)*, on the frontiers of Tibet, in a gathering place for the annual festivals[30]. The largest group of circular stone settings of this kind, with stones 2 or 3 metres in diameter, sometimes slightly ovoid in form, either with or without the central pillar, is in the mountains above Shapgeding *(Šab dge sdiṅs)* and on the road between Dopṭakdsong and Sakya: unfortunately the photographs of these sites were lost during the crossing of a river.

We shall have occasion to discuss later the problems presented by these sites. Are they tombs, or are they designed to mark out areas for some other purpose, or may they perhaps serve both these functions? Before considering these questions we must first refer to some other similar sites which have been discovered and also to the structures which have been identified as tombs. I myself have noted monolithic stelae on the plateau leading to Zhidekar *(gŽi sde mk'ar?)* in western Tibet[31], at Byi'u[32], near Lake Manasarovar, and, in the regions bordering on Tibet, at Garbyang[33] and Dopṭakdsong *(Plate 38)*.

Near Reting *(Rva sgreṅ)* is a rough circle of large stones *(phaong, p'a boṅ)*, on the top of which flutter streamers bearing printed prayers; the site is traditionally regarded as sacred to a Ḍākinī. Another ancient tomb, also circular in shape, was recorded by Georges de Roerich[34].

A site which shows some analogy with the one at Shapgeding is the *doring (rdo riṅ)* to the south of the salt lake of Pangongtsho *(sPaṅ goṅ mts'o)*. The name itself ("long stone") is very significant. Here Roerich[35] found eighteen parallel rows of standing stones, each row ending in a stone circle of large stones set vertically in the ground, with a kind of altar of undressed stone opposite each circle[36]. Within each circle were taller stones like those found at Pu, Dopṭakdsong and Garbyang. All the stones in the *doring* were aligned from east to west, and Roerich compares them with the megalithic alignments at Carnac in Brittany. It way well be that this site had a double significance: as a sacred place marked out and protected by the parallel lines of stones[37] and as a burial place.

As Mrs A.W. Macdonald, to whom we owe the first systematic study of this subject[38], has noted, other megalithic monuments were observed by Bacot in eastern Tibet[39].

In the village of Saga Roerich[40] discovered a large monolith of grey stone surrounded by pillars of white quartz. The surface of the large stone showed traces of butter: i.e., of offerings. Near the large salt lake of Danrayuntsho *(Dan rva yu mts'o?)* he also found megalithic structures consisting of standing stones surrounded by slabs arranged in a square. Nearby were tombs surrounded by stones arranged in square formation[41], aligned from east to west with a large stone at the east end — which seems to suggest that the body was laid with the head to the east. Roerich assigned these tombs to the megalithic period. This is an unduly vague dating; but since no excavations have been carried out it is impossible to establish the age of these tombs.

Stone settings with either one or three standing stones in the middle have been recorded in other parts of Tibet and Mongolia[42]; and the Ch'iang, who had already established themselves in the Kokonor region in the 2nd millennium B.C., also buried their dead in a kind of stone tomb[43].

Sporadic excavations carried out near Lhasa during the second world war by Dr Aufschnaiter, who had escaped from a prisoner-of-war camp and sought refuge in Tibet with his friend Harrer, led to the discovery of tombs and of pottery vessels. The tombs were of remarkably complex structure: the excavation reports note the occurrence of dressed stone and large boulders[44], of enclosure walls[45] and of tumuli[46]. The dead were buried in recesses hollowed out of the rock, with stone closure slabs, or laid in a kind of shaft grave *(a pozzetto)*; and the finding of skulls and bones in pottery jars suggests that a second burial was carried out after the decomposition of the flesh. The same conclusion seems to emerge from the examination of the tomb at Site XII, where there is a double burial. The pottery is either handmade or wheel-thrown and is painted a brilliant red; but it is essentially atypical. The occurrence of charcoal suggests that the funeral rites were performed near the tombs and burial places.

Other tombs have been discovered near Leh *(sLeh)* in Ladakh[47]: they were covered with stone slabs and the interiors were built of undressed stones, in the form of walls. I cannot accept Francke's view that the tombs were originally above ground level; for since the excavations were carried out by inexpert operators it is impossible to establish whether there was another grave above the tomb proper, as in the tombs found in Swat and the Indus valley. The tombs were some 1.80 metres long, 1.40 metres wide and 1.80 metres deep. The pottery was hand-made, not wheel-thrown, and the largest vessel, found in a fragmentary condition, seems to have been not more than 95 cm high and wide. Some jars were decorated with patterns in dark red; the excavator does not, however, record the ground colour[48].

A second series of excavations produced no painted pottery; the decoration, consisting only of incised lines, was similar to that on pottery discovered farther west, at Balukhar *(Ba lu mk'ar?)*, Alchi and other sites, in patterns of zigzags, ladders and other motifs which may represent leaves or grasses. In each tomb were found numbers of skulls — from three to fifteen or twenty — of dolichocephalic type, in contrast with the brachycephalic skulls which predominate in the present population. Various bronze objects were also found, including oblong beads of the length and girth of a finger and bell-shaped pendants with triangular apertures and a suspension ring at the top. Among other objects recovered were beads of glass paste, some bronze fragments interpreted by Francke as parts of a mirror, a seal with a cross motif similar to those found in Iran, a bronze vessel, bracelets and even some small pieces of iron. Francke dates the tombs to around 500 B.C., but there is insufficient evidence either to support or to reject his view.

Francke's conclusions are very debatable, and his description of the tombs and the material recovered does not provide a basis for reaching any positive view. It seems to me beyond doubt, however, that the finds as he describes them show considerable similarities to the material recovered in Swat and particularly along the banks of the Indus, which can be attributed to the Dards — the people who are known to have made their way along the Indus valley to Leh, and perhaps beyond this; in Khalatse *(K'a la rtse ?)*, Hanupat and other areas in Ladakh until quite recently — I cannot speak for the present situation — Dard dialects were spoken alongside Tibetan and the local form of Tibetan incorporated numerous Dard words.

Nor can I accept Francke's suggestion that the archaeological evidence reflects the existence of funeral rites similar to those still practised, in which the body is quartered and cut into small pieces; for in these rites the bones are broken and the skull does not remain intact.

The area with which we are here concerned was, as already noted, connected with Tibet by events which took place in the historical period (7th century A.D.), although the full tibetanisation of Ladakh was not finally achieved until a much later period (9th century); and the oldest ethnic stock in Ladakh is largely alien to that of Tibet.

On the basis of the evidence recorded by Francke Roerich agrees that the skulls found are dolichocephalic, whereas the population of present-day Ladakh is brachycephalic. His own observations suggest that the dolichocephalic type is found on the borders of Tibet proper, while the brachycephalic type predominates in central Tibet, the Brahmaputra valley and South-East Asia. Roerich believes that the tombs in Ladakh which are known locally as "nomads' tombs" are indeed characteristic of the nomad peoples, the Horpa. All this, however, is still problematic.

The circular tombs surrounded by stones are never found in large groups: usually three or four together, as in the Tibetan part of Nepal *(Plate 40)*, at Shapgeding and in the areas visited by Roerich[49]. It is interesting to note that objects decorated in what is now generally known as the "animal style" and small ribbed arrows like those published by Roerich[50] were found in these areas.

Another tomb surrounded by stones, oblong in plan, is found at high altitude near the Ḍölma *(sGrol ma)* pass, not far from Mount Kailāsa. This is the tomb commonly known as the "Tomb of the Ascetic". Whether or not it is of Buddhist origin, it is undoubtedly a place of recognised sanctity, for visiting pilgrims are accustomed to tear off a piece of their clothing and deposit it in token of homage[51] *(Plate 39)*.

To these various pieces of evidence must be added certain other chance discoveries about which I have been unable to obtain detailed information. Thus during the construction of a road near Gyamda *(rGya mda')* a tomb containing the remains of a body was discovered. It is not recorded whether any pottery was found with the body, but the interesting feature was the discovery of a circular turquoise, similar to one said to have been found in a tomb at Nachukha *(Nag c'u k'a)*. I take this information from H.E. Richardson[52], who suggests that these turquoises may represent the *ke ke ru* which is referred to in the chronicles of Tun huang[53] as the badge of rank of a particular officer. Jäschke defines the *ke ke ru* in his dictionary as "a white precious stone", which seems to indicate something similar to the jade circles found in early Chinese tombs. In the absence of exact information, however, it is not possible to reach any definite conclusion[54].

Another site of megalithic type — though here again the term must be used with caution — is found on the Kanzam pass leading into Spiti. On this wide pass, with almost the dimensions of a plateau, are a number of standing stones, most of which have collapsed or been displaced by the snow; a considerable number, however, are still *in situ*. This is not merely a *lhatho (lha t'o)*, one of the cairns which are still regularly erected on the highest points of mountain passes, but a considerable area entirely covered with large slabs of stone and boulders, similar to the site at Saga to which Roerich refers. It must be remembered that the cult of mountains was formerly one of the commonest forms of religious expression in Tibet. The pass might thus be both a place of propitiation for travellers and a place of sacred significance to the local tribes. Here there might be standing stones used for the deposit of offerings or for seasonal festivals; and it is also possible that the chiefs of the tribe were buried in this area, their tribal ancestor being identified with the mountain or with the god who in some previous age had descended there. In places such as this, therefore, there may well have been a number of different factors in play, serving various purposes but combining to give the site a unique sacred significance.

While Pu and Garbyang are undoubtedly cult sites, the same function cannot be assigned to the enclosures marked out by lines of stones. The occurrence in close proximity to one another of similar stone circles, as at Lo and Shapgeding[55], suggests that these are in fact burial places: cf. the stone circles of the Kafirs and the Laghman area of Afghanistan. It is also significant that until quite recent times *(Plates 41, 42)* the practice of building stone enclosures to protect the dead — admittedly not circular in form — was found in Tibet.

I conclude, therefore, that a distinction must be drawn between circular or square structures with a central pillar or *doring (rdo riṅ)* and those without a *doring*. It seems very likely that stone circles without a *doring* are in fact tombs; but confirmation of this could be obtained only by excavation.

The presence of a *doring* or central standing stone gives the structure a different character, conveying a ritual significance. This can be illustrated by the *doring* of Ḍalha *(dGra lha)* at Pu[56], or by the standing stone with the offerings of butter referred to on page 52 above. In this last case, however, the libations and offerings of butter may not only perpetuate a very ancient tradition but may also reflect a practice which has grown up in recent times in virtue of the sanctity attributed to structures whose original purpose has been forgotten. We also know from the chronicles of Tun huang[57] that it was common practice to set up a stone when swearing fidelity to someone or concluding an agreement. Clearly, therefore, we are faced with problems of great complexity for which, in the present state of knowledge, no solution can be offered.

Nor can we exclude the possibility that the stones standing by themselves in the centre of a circle may be *semata* — marks indicating the position of a grave for the purpose of the funeral rites which were periodically performed. The existence of *semata* over tombs is attested, for example, in prehistoric and protohistorical burial places in Swat.

Reference must also be made here to the religious shrines of the Bonpo. We cannot get any impression of what these were like from modern examples, which are on the Buddhist model. The ancient Bonpo shrines were not known as *lhakhang (lha k'aṅ)*, like the Buddhist ones, but as *sekhang (gsas k'aṅ)*, from *gsas*, a word of sacred significance to the Bonpo. We do not know what they were like, but to judge from the remains which have been discovered, particularly those found at Khyunglung in western Tibet — regarded as one of the most sacred places of the Bonpo religion, the supposed residence of its founder — the temple was apparently circular[58].

On the basis of all this evidence it has been suggested that there existed in Tibet a megalithic proto-culture developed out of Neolithic traditions which moved along two routes: one leading through the corridor of the Euro-Asiatic steppe in the Kokonor region into central Tibet and perhaps extending into Tsang, the other running into Kashmir and Spiti[59]. The material available is not yet sufficient to permit any firm conclusions.

The most reliable archaeological evidence and the best dating material is, of course, provided by pottery; but in Tibet this evidence, so essential for establishing even an approximate chronology, is not available, since it has not yet been possible to carry out any proper scientific excavations. We have already seen that no positive indications can be drawn from the pottery found at Leh or discovered by Aufschnaiter.

We are thus left without any reliable information about the ancient pottery of Tibet. Travellers and scholars have concerned themselves with modern Tibetan pottery, not with material recovered by excavation. Given the traditionalism of Tibetan art, it is of course possible that the modern pottery goes back to ancient models; but Tibet's many contacts with neighbouring countries and in particular the influence of metal vessels, which frequently show a blending of Chinese and Indian features, make it impossible to reach any conclusion[60].

As we have seen, the Lepchas believed that they had come down from the mountains; and they also believed that they would return there by way of an underground passage[61] or mount to the sky by way of a tower. Although jars have been discovered from which it was thought that such a tower may have been built up, I have not myself seen any. R. de Nebesky-Wojkowitz[62] had not himself seen any either, but gives a description (without any drawings) on the basis of some types which had come to his notice. He also records that when the Daramdin plateau was being brought into cultivation the remains of a stone tower were discovered[63]. On the pottery he has this to say:

"For the most part it consists of small sherds, the edges of which show much rounding and smoothing. The clay, with an admixture of mica, shows colour variations from reddish brown to blackish grey according to the firing. The fragments come from vessels of very varying size, including small thin-walled bowls with everted rims and jars of some size with walls several centimetres thick... The great majority of the material has no decoration: a few pieces have three dark bands running horizontally round the outside of the mouth, and one fragment has a barely distinguishable incised dog-tooth pattern, uncoloured."

A further question, which would merit fuller discussion if better examples were available, is raised by the rock carvings found in Ladakh, in the Tsang area in western Tibet, and on the eastern borders of the country. The carvings, produced by pecking with stones on granite boulders, usually represent animals, including particularly ibexes, men on horseback, armed men fighting and, at a later period, *chötens* (see below, p. 96)[64]. Some of them, particularly in western Tibet, are accompanied by dedicatory inscriptions which can be dated to the early days of Buddhism in Tibet. Carvings of this kind are so common in Asia, however, that we cannot draw any valid conclusions about their origin or about the interplay of influences between one area and another.

THE HISTORICAL PERIOD

II

The Royal Tombs

The royal tombs at Yarlung, near Chonggye *(aP'yoṅ rgyas)*, are monuments of particular importance which merit extended discussion; they were ranked by the Tibetans themselves as an obligatory place of pilgrimage. With them we enter a well defined historical period, in virtue both of the reliability of the traditions relating to the tombs and the existence of inscriptions which confirm the dating of at least some of them.

I visited these tombs in 1948[65] and published the first study of them, which may be referred to for fuller details. Further studies were published by H.E. Richardson, who was for several years head of the British mission in Lhasa, remaining there until 1950.

The largest tomb is that of Songtsengampo *(Sroṅ btsan sgam po)*, known as the Bangsomarpo *(Baṅ so dmar po)*, who died in 649. Near this tomb are tumuli belonging to other kings. Since after the triumph of Buddhism these tombs were visited by large numbers of pilgrims we have a number of accounts of them by later writers, but we also have certain older texts which enable us to deduce how the tombs — or at least some of them — were built. The mound of Songtsengampo, like others in its immediate vicinity, stood on a large square base which was probably used for the ritual procession *(pradakṣiṇa)* associated with any sacred building. Alternatively, as the Chinese chronicles indicate[66], it may have been planted with trees. *Plate 44* shows a circular cavity marking the position of the tumulus: this may be the result of the violation of the royal tombs in the time of Khonsher *(K'on bžer)*, in 866. This confirms what we can deduce from the tradition — if not contemporary, at any rate based on ancient sources — that large quantities of precious objects were buried along with the king. The burial did not take place immediately after death, but was delayed for a year or more until the body had been mummified (or perhaps had been allowed to decompose) in a place set apart for that purpose.

Songtsengampo's tomb contained either nine or five chambers[67], square in plan. In the central chamber was placed a silver coffin containing the body, covered with gilding, and round it were laid various objects which had belonged to the king, his garments and his treasures. Above some of the tombs, for example that of Thidesongtsen *(K'ri lde sroṅ brtsan, 755–797)*, was set a pillar *(Plate 46)*. This pillar, which is also found above other tombs *(Plate 45)*, had of course symbolic significance: it represented the *axis mundi*, giving visible form to the idea of communication between different planes (the subterranean, the ethereal and the celestial) and thus expressing the correspondence between microcosm and macrocosm, the similitude between the residence of the sovereign (now his tomb) and the universe. According to mK'yen brtse[68], there was in his day a bas-relief carving of Songtsengampo on his tomb; but when I visited the tomb in 1948 there was no trace of this.

When proper excavation is undertaken it will no doubt — in spite of the damage done by tomb robbers — throw light on the interesting problem of the structure of the tombs, both externally and internally. It would be important to establish, for example, whether there was a veranda in front of the tomb, or alternatively a series of rooms for performing the various ceremonies of the funerary cult which were repeated at regular intervals after the king's death. The tradition records that a royal minister (Nanglön, *Naṅ blon*) resided permanently near the tomb[69].

We know from ancient rituals discovered in Central Asia that the ceremonies were elaborate and complex. They included sacrifices of animals and also human sacrifices[70], which would imply the existence of appropriate ritual structures associated with the tombs. It is likely that, as in the case of the

Siberian tombs excavated by Rudenko, the tomb robbers would take only objects of value, leaving other things which were of no interest to them but may nevertheless be of great importance to Tibetan archaeology.

The other tombs are grouped round that of Songtsengampo. Some of them have inscriptions, like the tomb of Ṭhidesongtsen *(K'ri lde sroṅ brtsan)*[71] *(Plate 46)*. On the pillar above Ṭhidesongtsen's tomb are carvings executed by pecking with a stone: a swastika and a crude representation of a face. These are not, however, contemporary with the tomb but are graffiti left by pilgrims of a later period.

The practice of erecting tombs and mounds, with or without a pillar, certainly did not originate with Songtsengampo: according to a tradition which appears to me credible it dates from the reign of Ḍigumtsenpo *(Gri gum brtsan po)*, when Tibetan religious beliefs underwent considerable changes. Digumtsenpo's tomb is thought to be at Ngarpathang *(Ṅar pa t'aṅ)*, near Yarlung[72].

It may be noted that tombs had a distinctive name, a secret name which varied according to the king.

The royal tombs reflect funeral practices which were no doubt followed also by the nobility. Some noble families, particularly those from which the kings chose their wives, enjoyed particular importance, frequently coming into conflict with the royal power. We can be certain that members of these families had tombs similar to those of the kings; but here again we are confronted with a problem which archaeologists of the future must seek to solve by identifying other mounds round Yarlung, Lhasa and other centres and carrying out proper excavations.

Apart from the tombs themselves other evidence on the period of the Tibetan kings is provided by the inscriptions carved on pillars. A special section of Tibetan archaeology must therefore be devoted to epigraphy. We already have a number of these inscriptions, for example the one on Thidesongtsen's tomb; the one at Samye *(bSam yas)* which I have published, an edict proclaiming Buddhism as the state religion *(Plate 43)*; and others at Karchung *(sKar c'uṅ)* and Tshurphu *(mTs'ur p'u)*. The best known of these inscriptions is the one on the pillar *(rdo riṅ)* in front of the western gate of the Tsuglagkhang in Lhasa, which commemorates a treaty between Mu tsung and Thitsukdetsen *(K'ri gtsug lde brtsan)* in 821-822[73]. There are two other pillars with inscriptions dating from 804 to 812, during the reign of Thidesongtsen, in the monastery of Zhailhakhang *(Žva'i lha k'aṅ)*[74]; and there is another, dating from the reign of Thisongdetsen, at Demosa *(bDe mo sa)* on the north bank of the Tsangpo[75].

In addition to these inscriptions preserved on monuments which have withstood the ravages of time there are others, now lost, which have been faithfully preserved in various literary works. It is quite possible that some of these may yet come to light again.

Civil and Military Architecture

Tibetan civil and military architecture went through a gradual process of development after the establishment of the dynasty and the introduction of Buddhism. According to the ancient Chinese sources the Tibetans led a pastoral and nomadic life in early times, without any fixed settlements. The places where they set up their tents were frequently surrounded by protective walls *(rva, ra)*, the prototype of the *chag-ri (lcags ri)*, the "iron wall", which provides protection for temples and the large monasteries and was adopted under the influence of Buddhist cosmography. The same sources

49

50

51 →

52, 53

54, 55

56, 57

speak of flat-roofed houses — i.e. dwellings of the same type as present-day Tibetan houses[76] — which sometimes reached a height of several metres. Nevertheless we know, again on the evidence of the texts, that the nobles also lived in tents. In winter they sought refuge in their houses, but in summer, when they followed their subjects (still largely involved in a nomadic way of life) and their flocks and herds over the plateaux, they camped out in tents. The kings and the most powerful families — as we can still see from the ruined towns of Tsaparang and Chang — owned large castles or palaces *(sku mk'ar,* or simply *mk'ar)*. According to the traditions of the Bon religion which preceded Buddhism, each king had his own palace; and when the king died his successor abandoned the previous royal residence and built a new one of his own, in the same way as he appointed a new minister and a chief priest.

Since the royal dynasty originated in Yarlung it is not surprising that the remains of some of the most ancient and most famous buildings of Tibet have been found in this area. Among them is Yumbulhakhar *(Yum bu lha mk'ar)*, also known as *Yum bu gla sgam* or *Um bu rdsaṅs mk'ar* in the chronicles of Ladakh *(Plate 48)*, said to have been built by a king (perhaps not entirely legendary) to whose reign the first appearance of Buddhism in Tibet is traditionally dated. Like other places hallowed by a long religious tradition, and perhaps also on account of its site, this castle still exists; and indeed the present building is said to be the original structure, its slender tower with its pagoda-type roof *(rgya p'ugs)* soaring proudly above a range of lower buildings.

In the course of an expedition to Tibet in 1948 I visited this castle and carried out a careful survey. All round it are remains which suggest that there were once a series of much larger buildings on the spur of this rocky hill. The walls are constructed of rectangular stones, with occasional traces of earth mortar. The buildings are much later than the date attributed to them by tradition. They have apparently been rebuilt several times after destruction by war or the ravages of time, invariably on the same site — perhaps because of the tradition attached to the site, perhaps also because it is the most suitable place for a watchtower commanding the valley. The method of construction is the same as at Chingpataktse *(P'yiṅ pa sTag rtse)*, the former capital of the kings of Yarlung, near the present-day town of Chongye. The remains are extremely imposing, with towers and high walls protecting the palaces, all constructed of roughly dressed stones and sun-dried bricks, of the type found all over Central Asia, Afghanistan and Iran, where the dry climate gives this type of construction the necessary solidity and permanence.

The towers, designed for defensive purposes, as watch-towers or as signal stations for use in war, go back to very early times. They are mentioned in the early Chinese sources[77], which tell us that the whole country was covered with these towers, set at a distance of 10 *li* (576 metres) apart.

From the time of Songtsengampo, the real founder of Tibetan power, there was a great flowering of architecture; but unfortunately our only knowledge of its achievements comes from the literary tradition or from the few surviving remains. Tradition attributes to this king the building of a nine-storied palace at Phaongkha *(P'a boṅ k'a)*[78]. Near Samye are Ṭakmar *(aBrag dmar)*, the birthplace of Ṭhisongdetsen *(K'ri sroṅ lde brtsan)*, and Yamalung *(gYa' ma luṅ)*[79]; not far away was Zurkhar *(Zur mk'ar* or *Zuṅ mk'ar)*; and just above the monastery of Samye was *Has po ri*. All these sites, however, are in a state of total ruin. The five *chötens*[80] near Zurkhar built to commemorate the spot where according to tradition the king met Padmasaṃbhava have clearly been rebuilt at a later date which cannot be exactly established. The Marpori *(dMar po ri)*, said to have been built by Songtsengampo, had eleven stories. Ushangdo *(U šaṅ rdo* or *On caṅ rdo)*, where there was also a temple, was begun by Ṭhidesongtsen *(K'ri lde sroṅ brtsan)* and completed by Repachen *(Ral pa can)*; it had nine stories. Chinese archaeologists will therefore have to turn their attention to the areas round Yarlung, Samye and Lhasa. For the moment we must perforce confine ourselves to the limited amount of established information we possess, recognising that we have no plans or surveys nor any clear idea of the building methods adopted in the different periods.

When we recall the antagonisms between China and Tibet, the frequent conflicts between the royal family and the aristocracy, the struggles between powerful families for land and grazing rights, the emergence of various local overlords and, at a later date, the quarrels between monasteries, it is easy to see why military architecture developed in Tibet. Its typical expression was the fortified residence, the castle with towers and other defensive structures whose remains are found all over the country *(Plates 50-52)*[81], particularly on the slope of a hill or the summit of a pass, guarding the entrance to a defile or commanding a valley. The towers are round *(Plate 53)* or more usually square. They were watch-towers on the borders of the territory of the most powerful families during the troubled period which followed the fall of the Tibetan dynasty and lasted until the great abbeys asserted their supremacy in the 12th and 13th centuries, or defensive towers belonging to such minor potentates as the Sakyapa, when Tibet came under the nominal control of the Mongols, and later the Phagmoṭupa *(P'ag mo gru pa)*.

As an example we may take the tower built by Milarepa at the behest of Marpa — although, as Wylie has shown, later religious tradition piously concealed the real motives, the practical and territorial reasons, for its construction. The tower *(Plate 49)*, known as the Sekharguthok *(Sras mk'ar dgu t'og)*[82], went through three successive stages — veranda type, round tower and semicircular tower — before reaching its final square shape. It is said to have had nine stories[83], like the palace of the kings of Ladakh, which is however much later, having been built in the time of *Seṅ ge rnam rgyal* (c. 1640–1645). Examples of round towers can be seen in other parts of Tibet, for example at Penam *(sPa nam* or *snam) (Plate 52)*.

The country is littered with remains of this kind *(Plates 56, 57)*, which we shall not be able to assign to particular periods until proper excavations have been carried out and have yielded dating material. They are all built in the same fashion, either with rectangular blocks of stone jointed with earth mortar or with natural boulders closely bonded together *(Plate 57)*. In later periods the blocks are less carefully squared, but the gaps between them are filled with fragments struck off during the dressing of the stone and the solidity of the structure is maintained by the increased thickness of the walls. Another type of construction is also found, using large blocks of earth tempered with straw and hardened in the sun; these blocks are sometimes over a metre long and more than 50 cm thick.

Marpa's tower, like the tower at Yumbulhakhar already mentioned, has a pagoda roof of Chinese type *(rgya p'ugs)* — an architectural feature which does not appear to be attested in any surviving structures earlier than the Sakyapa period.

There are also quite a number of apsidal buildings, including in particular the *lhakhang* of Jampel *(ɑJam dpal)* at Samye, which has some analogy with the temple at Sirkap (Taxila), and another at Kampadsong *(sGam pa rdsoṅ) (Plate 55)*. The latter is a semicircular structure similar to one of the earlier phases of Marpa's tower. Castles were naturally less carefully finished than temples *(Plate 57)*[84], but it is undeniable that the sites selected for these buildings and their imposing size gave an impression of great strength, particularly when considered in the light of the means of warfare then available *(Plates 56-58)*.

The building technique which can be very approximately described as Gandharan appears in a number of *chötens* found in the Tholing *(mT'o gliṅ)* area and elsewhere in western Tibet. This is characterised by the use of irregularly shaped blocks, carefully dressed on the outer surface, laid in regular courses and alternating with rectangular stones of different length but about the same height; the gaps which are liable to occur in this type of construction are filled with flat stones and small fragments. This method remained in use for a long period in the construction of larger buildings; and even when sun-dried bricks were used for the walls the foundation courses were almost invariably of stone. In buildings constructed entirely of unbaked brick *(Plate 54)* the bricks were laid in courses, fitting closely together. Sometimes courses of bricks alternated with courses of stone and rubble. The walls of castles might have triangular loopholes *(Plate 50)*.

Finally mention must be made of the bridges, sometimes constructed of wood, either of cantilever or suspension type, the latter in particular being marvels of bold engineering *(Plate 59)*.

Temples

Although they have been frequently altered, destroyed and rebuilt in the course of centuries, the earliest temples seem to have been of relatively small size. In general they were very similar to the temples built in the 10th and 11th centuries, at the time of the revival of Buddhism. According to a tradition which is universally accepted by the Tibetans but seems to me of somewhat questionable authenticity, the two oldest temples are the Ṭhulnang *(aP'rul snaṅ)*, built by the Nepalese wife of Songtsengampo, who died in 649, and the Ramoche *(Ra mo c'e)*, built by his Chinese wife. The

Ṭhulnang is referred to in the inscriptions recorded by a Tibetan source[85] without any founder's name, while the Ramoche is said to have been built by "the Chinese woman" — whom I believe to have been Princess Chin Ch'eng, wife of Ṭhisongdetsen's father (755–797?). Whatever the period of their foundation, however, it is unquestionable that in the course of centuries both of these temples have undergone restorations which have altered their original form. The temple of Katse *(sKa ts'al)* at Maldo *(Mal gro)*[86], also attributed to Songtsengampo's Nepalese wife, is quite small, as are the temples at Keru[87] and Ṭhanṭuk *(K'ra ạbrug)*[88]; the latter is also attributed to Songtsengampo but, like the Ramoche, it is very probably to be dated to the reign of Ṭhisongdetsen, his descendant. But whatever their exact dating all these temples are certainly among the oldest sacred buildings in Tibet, even though they may not have come down to us in their original condition.

A recent Chinese publication[89] reproduces two panels, one representing an elephant (one of the "seven jewels" of traditional Buddhist iconography), the other an episode from the life of Buddha showing the Bodhisattva on horseback accompanied by a servant carrying an umbrella. The book dates these precious fragments very broadly to the T'ang period. I myself tried to take photographs of the panels, but my photographer, a Sikkimese, was somewhat inexpert and the light was very poor: he did his best with the help of a number of paraffin lamps, but the result was something less than perfect. Nevertheless in view of the great importance of the work I reproduce a detail *(Plate 109)* showing the Bodhisattva cutting his hair after giving up his princely way of life. Another scene, not reproduced in this book, shows the Bodhisattva so deeply absorbed in meditation that two children who are putting straws into his ears are unable to distract him. The most important feature of these panels, however, is that they bear an inscription which on palaeographic grounds can be dated to the 12th century. Unfortunately the name of the king is illegible – all that can be read is *mahārājādhirāja bhaṭṭā-*

raka; but the inscription at least shows beyond doubt that this is a Nepalese work which has no connection with China.

We know of at least one embellishment to the Jokhang. It was due to the liberality and piety of a king of western Tibet, Ripumalla, who caused the *ütok (dbu t'og)* of the temple — a term applied either to the roof or to an attic storey — to be rebuilt in gold. Ripumalla lived about the end of the 13th century[90]. We cannot, however, exclude the possibility that in the very earliest days of Buddhism other Buddhist rulers of neighbouring countries may have enlarged or even completely rebuilt the temple.

The statue now to be seen in the Tsuglagkhang appears to have nothing in common with the original, which had previously been in the Ramoche. The central part of the temple, however, is undoubtedly ancient, although it shows later additions; and careful examination of the chapels round the main *cella* reveals traces of very ancient paintings, largely covered or masked by later work, some of which can be dated to the time of the fifth Dalai Lama (1617–1682) or Sanghyeghyatsho *(Sans rgyas rgya mts'o)*, who was elected regent in 1679. The *apsaras* depicted on the capitals have nothing Chinese about them and appear to be related to the artistic schools of the countries bordering on Kashmir like Swat, Kulu and Chambā — in all of which there was a long tradition of craftsmanship in wood. This is true also of the wooden veranda, in which the beams with representations of animal or human heads clearly belong to the same tradition[91]: counterparts can be found, for example, at Iwang[92]. All this suggests either that the building went through several successive phases or that craftsmen from different countries and trained in different artistic traditions were working on it at the same time.

The Chinese publication already referred to contains a photograph[93] of a group of statues representing Songtsengampo and his Nepalese and Chinese queens which are found also, with slight variations, in the Tsuglagkhang and the Potala. These works do not belong to any clearly defined artistic schools, and the Tibetans themselves consider them as having been supernaturally created. In my view, however, one of them clearly shows striking resemblances to a statue *(Plate 69)*[94] which formerly stood in a temple at Tiak in western Tibet founded by Rinchensangpo: I cannot be sure whether the temple is still standing, for when I visited it the building was already in a state of ruin. It seems possible to detect some connection with certain artistic traditions of Kashmir (Ushkur), a kind of distant echo of some Gandharan stucco work[95]. If this were true it would provide confirmation of the tradition recorded in the literary sources that the kings of western Tibet were involved in the enlargement or rebuilding of the temples of Lhasa. This rebuilding may have taken place at an even earlier period than the reign of Ripumalla, coinciding with a revival of the Buddhist faith after a period of decadence lasting perhaps a generation.

Another area in which there is much scope for proper scientific investigation is the region round Lhasa, on both banks of the River Kyichu *(sKyid c'u)*. In addition to the mounds which have already been discussed there are two temples at Karchung *(sKar c'uṅ)* built respectively by Ṭhisongdetsen and Repachen, both subsequently destroyed and rebuilt, which would repay careful examination; and there is a pillar at Karchung with an inscription of great historical importance dating from the period of the temple's foundation[96]. Beyond Karchung, also on the left bank of the Kyichu, is Ushangdo *(U šaṅ rdo* or *On caṅ rdo)*, with another famous temple founded by Repachen and restored at a later period. Round the temple are four *chötens* which do not look particularly old but may conceal traces of much more ancient structures; the two pillars *(rdo riṅ)* associated with the temple *(Plates 66, 67)*, one outside and the other inside, bear no inscriptions. Near the confluence of the Kyichu and the Tsangpo, at Sinpori *(Srin po ri)*, is another important temple which is traditionally attributed to a celebrated Indian teacher named Vibhūticandra[97]; nothing remains of the original structure but a pillar *(rdo riṅ)* without inscriptions and a very beautiful stone lamp.

61, 62

63, 64

68 ↑   69   70

71, 72, 73

There are of course certain exceptions to the general statements made above about the temples built during the first and second stages in the introduction of Buddhism. Two particularly important exceptions are the temples at Samye *(Plate 63)* and Tholing *(Plate 65)*. The former was built by Ṭhisongdetsen when Buddhism was proclaimed the official religion of Tibet; the decree announcing this was inscribed rather crudely on a pillar in front of the temple *(Plate 43)*[98]. The latter is in western Tibet, and will be discussed further below.

The temple at Samye — of which we have a very early description, if not quite contemporary with its construction — is a large complex, several stories high, with eight buildings aligned on the cardinal points and intermediate points set round the central temple. These eight outer buildings clearly represent the eight continents (four large and four small) of Buddhist cosmology which lie round the Jambudvīpa on which we live and on which the Buddha Śākyamuni was born. In other words, the central idea of the Samye temple is to represent a microcosm which is a projection of the macrocosm. The intention was to put in place of the old world, dominated by powers which Buddhism regarded as demoniac, a new world in which a central place was occupied in religious ceremonies by the Chögyel *(C'os rgyal)*, the "king according to the Law": Ṭhisongdetsen *(K'ri sroṅ lde btsan)*, who had introduced Buddhism into Tibet. At the four corners are four *chötens* of different colours, erected by four ministers.

The whole of the area round Samye is thus of great importance for Tibetan archaeology, although the vicissitudes of time and the effects of a fire have destroyed much of the original structure.

According to Tibetan tradition many ancient temples were built in imitation of Indian models: Ramoche on the model of Vikramaśīlā, Samye and Tholing in imitation of Otantapuri. Even Depung *(aBras spuṅs)*, although belonging to a much later period, was believed to be modelled on the equally famous temple at Dhānyakaṭaka. Our sources also refer to the simultaneous occurrence of different styles in the same building: we are told, for example, that in the Samye temple and in the nine-storied palace of Muṭhitsenpo *(Mu k'ri brtsan po)* near the temple each storey was built by craftsmen from different countries working in different styles — Tibetan, Chinese, Khotanese and Indian. Statements of this kind, however, probably refer to the statues and perhaps to the wall paintings with which each storey is decorated[99]. Only proper excavation, by clearing the ancient foundations, will make it possible to establish whether the tradition has any basis in fact.

After the persecution of Buddhists by Langdarma *(Glaṅ dar ma)*, who died in 842, Tibet went through a very troubled period; but Buddhism continued to survive on the eastern confines of the country and recovered ground in western Tibet as a result of the teaching of Rinchensangpo *(Rin c'en bzaṅ po)*. In this period numbers of small communities grew up round a teacher and a modest chapel of the type discussed above. It appears, however, that the *doring* now fell out of use: the latest example known of a *doring* with inscriptions is the one at Gyellhakhang *(rGyal lha k'aṅ)*, which was largely destroyed by Godan's Mongols in 1240; it was set up by Nanam Dorjewangchuk *(sNa nam rDo rje dbaṅ p'yug, 976–1060)*, whose family, one of the oldest and noblest in Tibet, had frequently contracted matrimonial alliances with the kings. The temple, some 40 km north-west of Lhasa, was visited by H.E. Richardson, who discovered a pillar of ancient type with an inscription, partly damaged, referring to the decline of the Law and calling on the faithful to observe in the letter and the spirit its injunctions, which alone brought salvation[100].

We have very few specimens of the temple architecture of this second period, the rest having been damaged or destroyed during the intestine conflicts which threw Tibet into turmoil for several centuries. The best surviving examples are the temples in western Tibet which a credible tradition attributes to Rinchensangpo and his immediate successors, and which can be compared with the temples already referred to at Iwang, Samada and Nesar *(gNas gsar)* in the Tsang region and at Ḍanang, to the south of the Tsangpo[101]. In general these temples are small, and rectangular in plan *(Plate 64)*; frequently, but not invariably, there is an atrium with wooden pillars in front of the temple. Inside, in front of the rear wall, is the altar, with the image to which the temple is dedicated *(gtso bo)*. The altar stands clear of the wall so that the visitor can walk round the statue which stands on it: the ritual required that in doing this he should keep the statue on his right. Sometimes the temple consists of two parts, one inside the other, separated by a passage running round the inner chamber in which the worshipper could perform the prescribed circuit. This type of architecture, the forerunner of the great monasteries and abbeys of later periods, is found all over Tibet. The plans followed the general types shown in figures (a), (b) and (c) on pp. 95–96. The interior was almost always decorated with paintings, some good examples of which, dating from the period of construction of the temples, have been preserved. The most important of these is Mangnang *(Maṅ naṅ)*[102], from which a translator *(lotsāva)*, not otherwise identified, took his name.

Accordingly Mangnang is a monument of outstanding importance in the history of Tibetan art[103]. It comprises an upper part, known to the caravaneers as Khardsong *(mK'ar rdsoṅ)* and Üssukhar *(dBus su mk'ar)*, "the castle in the middle", and a lower part consisting of fourteen temples *(lha k'aṅ)*, mostly in ruins, known as the Monastery of the *Lotsāva* of Mangnang. The paintings in these buildings, which are now probably destroyed or badly damaged — for the condition of the *lhakhang* when I saw it was already critical — are of very great interest as being by a number of painters from Kashmir, no doubt summoned by the *lotsāva* or by Rin-

91

chensangpo. We know that several painters were involved, for it is easy to distinguish a number of different hands. The photographs of the paintings were taken in deplorable conditions, but in view of the importance of these works I think it worth while to reproduce them, as the only evidence we possess on a school of art about which we know nothing.

The figure of a *sādhu* in *Plate 114* shows considerable affinities with the *sādhus* depicted on terracottas from Harvan in Kashmir; and the monk with his left hand held in front of him is very similar to a fragment of a gilded bronze *tondo*, also of Kashmiri workmanship, from Chang in western Tibet[104]. Some of the paintings, however, show a striking use of colours and chiaroscuro, giving an impression of volume[105] which is fairly rare in Indian painting.

Of equal quality is the figure of an *apsaras*, which can stand comparison with its counterpart at Ajaṇṭā[106] and is perhaps even superior to it in the nobility of its forms and the elegance of its lines. The group of divinities reproduced in *Plate 122* is by another hand, no less skilled: the paintings are notable for a certain deformation of the figures, which are shown in frontal view.

Another interesting item, also found in western Tibet, is an ivory statue *(Plate 128)*, which is probably the actual figure mentioned by Rinchensangpo's biographers[107].

Work such as this provides indisputable evidence of Kashmiri influence in Tibet in the 10th and 11th centuries; and similar examples from a later period have been found at Alchi in Ladakh. The wooden figure of a goddess

(Plate 150) from this monastery is also the work of a Kashmiri artist. Rinchensangpo brought in many artists from Kashmir to work on the building and decoration of the chapels which he founded, and the names of some of them are recorded in the Tibetan sources, in more or less garbled form[108]. Mangnang is not the only place where we can identify work by these artists. There is, for example, a statue of Hevajra, made from the wood of the "tree of illumination" of which the biography speaks[109]; and of even greater significance are the temple doors of Tsaparang *(Plate 138)* and Tholing *(Plate 136)*, with various episodes from the life of the Buddha on the side panels, and two other fragments from Tabo, published by Francke and later by myself *(Plate 129)*[110], the style of which leaves no doubt about their Kashmiri origin. Western Tibet had, of course, trading and cultural connections with Kashmir over a long period.

In the Tsang region there are a number of temples which are of interest for the paintings, statues or fragments of statues they contain; much has been destroyed by the wars which have ravaged the area, but much still survives[111]. The most important of these are the temples at Samada *(Plate 74)*, Iwang and Nesar *(gNas gsar)*. The temple at Samada preserves an inscription in archaic script referring to its founder, Chölotö *(C'os blo gros,* Dharmamati*)*, a disciple of Rinchensangpo[112]. The inscription tells us that the statues were the work of an Indian of Brahmin stock *(bram ze rigs)* named Mati who came from *Pan tso ra*. He was responsible for the carving of three statues of *thukdams (t'ugs dam)* or protective divinities — Chenresik *(sPyan ras gzigs,* Avalokiteśvara, Padmapāṇi), Channadorje *(P'yag na rdo rje,* Vajrāpaṇi*)* and Jamyang *(aJam dbyaṅs,* Mañjughoṣa*)*.

Although, as the inscription indicates, a number of sculptors of different origins and language had found their way to Tsang and central Tibet at this period, it was Mati the master craftsman *(sku mk'an)* who found favour in the eyes of Zhönnuö *(gŽon nu 'od)* and was given the commission.

At the time of my first visit only the statue of Padmapāṇi still remained *(Plate 70)*, and by the time of my second journey it had been removed[113].

The difficulty of identifying the place of origin of the sculptor and the rather unusual style of the statue make it impossible to assign this work with confidence to any particular school. In my view any connection with Bengal or Nepal can be excluded; but if Panjora or Pancora corresponds to the present-day Bajaurā a connection with the Kulu school seems plausible[114].

It is easier to find affinities for the large *chöten*[115], a magnificent example of Kashmiri architecture extending its influence to neighbouring countries[116].

In the Iwang temple we are left only with the paintings, which we know from the accompanying inscriptions were executed in two different styles *(lugs)*, one Indian *(rgya lugs)* and the other Khotanese *(li lugs)*; and this statement is supported by a study of the paintings themselves.

The temples at Nesar, in the Tsang region, and Ḍanang, south of the Tsangpo[117], are also of interest. Although of larger size than those discussed so far, they are built on the same plan. Both temples are well preserved and do not appear to have been restored: as we see them today they may date from the 11th or 12th century. In place of the wall paintings with which the Ḍanang temple may originally have been decorated — although on the most careful examination I was unable to detect any traces — the figure of the Buddha on the rear wall is now flanked by figures, some 3 metres high, of the eight Bodhisattvas who form his retinue, wearing long cloaks copied from Sassanid fabrics[118].

As regards the method of construction of these temples, what has been said above about civil and military architecture is equally applicable.

It should be noted also that as the great monastic communities increased in importance and consolidated their political hegemony the monasteries grew larger, developing into veritable towns centred on the principal building in which the monks came together for their daily assemblies and the great religious festivals. New buildings were added — seminaries, colleges, residences for the abbots, new temples dedicated by the faithful or by the leaders of the monastery, who enjoyed great prestige and considerable resources, to various particular divinities. One of the oldest and most interesting examples of this development is the monastery of Sakya (11th–13th centuries) *(Plate 71)*, which exerted considerable political power and was exposed to influences from both Nepal and China. The great popularity of the pagoda-type roof or series of superimposed roofs — a feature of Chinese origin — undoubtedly began at this period, and it was only in the villages that the *lhakhangs* preserved their ancient character and their modest size.

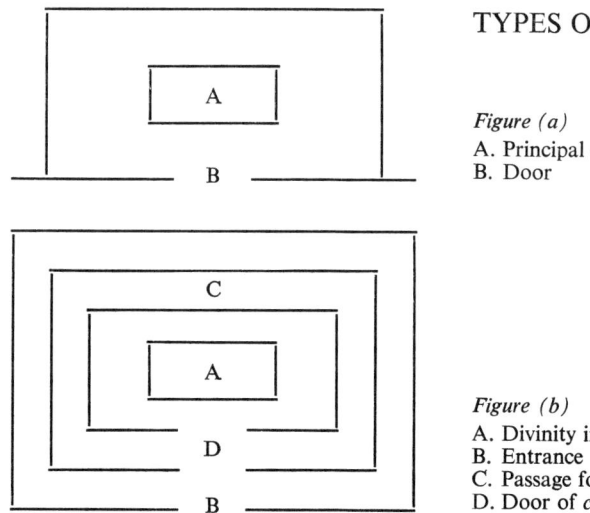

TYPES OF TEMPLE

Figure (a)
A. Principal divinity
B. Door

Figure (b)
A. Divinity in *cella*
B. Entrance
C. Passage for ritual circuit
D. Door of *cella*

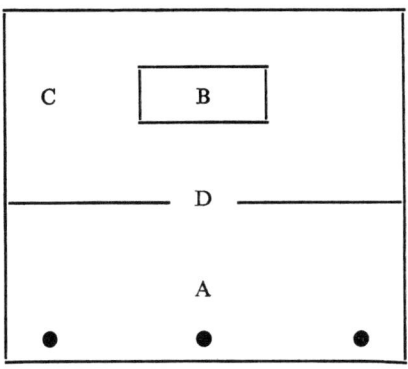

Figure (c)
A. Veranda with doors and pillars
B. Principal statue
C. *Cella*
D. Entrance to temple

There may also be a veranda in front of the temple of type (b). The walls are decorated with paintings, or alternatively with statues of standing or seated figures; in the latter case the statues are set on altars.

Chötens

One feature of Tibetan architecture which calls for particular discussion is the *chöten (mc'od rten)*, corresponding to the Indian *stūpa*. The *chöten*, which may vary in size according to circumstances, is a building of symbolic significance, a psycho-cosmogram like the *maṇḍala*[119], the body of the Law. It also has a functional rôle, since it may house the relics of saints — usually the ashes, but sometimes the whole body — or the remains of lamas who have enjoyed particular reputation during their life, or books or sacred objects which are no longer required for use but cannot be thrown away on account of the sacred character of the ceremonies in which they had been used.

The architecture of these *stūpas* is very variable. None of those I have seen in Tibet resembles the ancient *stūpas* — with a base, a dome and either

80

81

82

83

84

85

87

86

88

92

93

94

95

96

107

three or five "umbrellas" set at varying distances on the axis of the structure — like those at Bharhut and Sanchi, or even at Bodhnāth in Nepal.

Just as in the course of centuries Buddhism had gradually transformed its dogmatic structures, developing from the Lesser Vehicle to the Great Vehicle and then to the Tantric Vehicle which predominated in Tibet, so the form of the *stūpa* evolved. Its evolution took place, however, within the framework of certain accepted patterns which remained relatively stable, the standard of workmanship varying according to the skill of the builders.

The typology of the *chöten* covers a wide range. In theory, following literary traditions brought into Tibet from India, there are eight types, but no more than two or three are at all common[120]. The first of these is the *changchup-chöten (byaṅ c'ub mc'od rten)*, the "*chöten* of the Illumination". It has a square base with one or more steps round the foot; above this is a round drum, the *bum pa* or "pot"; above this again are either seven or thirteen "umbrellas", mounted on a central axis which traverses each of them; and at the top of the whole structure is a metal ring, usually gilded, supporting a crescent and circle which respectively represent the moon and the sun. The name for this last feature is *zla ñi* ("moon and sun") *(Plate 75)*. Structures of this kind gave expression to profound religious and mystical conceptions, varying according to the different schools. A second type of *chöten*, equally common, is the *lhapap (lha babs)*, the "descent from heaven", modelled on a building said to have been erected at Sāṃkāśya in India, on the very spot where Buddha descended from the heaven of Tuṣita, after visiting it to preach the Law to his mother, who had ascended thither after her death. The characteristic feature of this type of *chöten* is that on all four sides, or sometimes only on one, there are steps (the number may vary) enabling the visitor to climb up to the higher level on which the "pot" or "egg" (Sanskrit *aṇḍa*) is set and to walk round the *chöten*. In Tibet, however, the passage round the upper level is so narrow that it loses its functional rôle. This type was also imported from India and reflects very ancient traditions. The third of the commonest types of *chöten* is the *sgo mañ*, the "*chöten* with many doors", the most monumental form: in view of its importance this type is more fully discussed below.

Innumerable variants of these three types and of the other traditional models are found in Tibet, for apart from those at the great monasteries many *chötens* were built by nameless local craftsmen; and although the builders worked under the direction of lamas — themselves admittedly not always either expert or learned — they achieved only very approximate imitations of the classical models *(Plate 76)*. The *chötens* are almost invariably built of squared stones, sometimes in a style recalling the Gandharan building technique *(Plate 86)*, or of sun-dried brick with a plaster facing; the facing was frequently renewed, since this was regarded as a meritorious act. Since there is usually no dedicatory inscription it is not easy to establish the date of a *chöten*; but it may be possible to deduce its age from the *ts'a ts'as*[121] it contains. These are kept inside the "egg" or "pot", or on top of the base; they can sometimes be seen or handled, since there is a small window *(sgo)* in the "egg" or in the base itself. The custom of depositing *ts'a ts'as* in a *chöten* is derived from the Indian practice of having in some *stūpas* chests made of stone slabs, suitably protected and concealed from sight, inside which were reliquaries containing the remains of lamas who had died in the odour of sanctity, together with coins, necklaces and jewellery: material which offers a useful means of establishing at least the approximate date of the building.

The *chötens* must be regarded as temples; and it may be appropriate at this point to consider the various possible types of *ten (rten)*, "receptacle" or "container". These are the *ten* of the spirit, *thukten (t'ugs rten)* — although "spirit" is a very imperfect translation of the Tibetan *t'ugs* (= *sems* = Sanskrit *citta*), the ultimate spiritual essence, the void filled with light which is peculiar to the Buddha[122]; the *ten* of the body, *kuten (sku rten)*, that is, any representation of the Buddha, a Bodhisattva or a great lama; and the *ten* of the Word, *sungten (gsuṅ rten)*, meaning anything that is written, the words of Buddha, a book.

The *chöten* is thus fundamentally a *thukten:* it is a building designed to symbolise the ultimate essence of the Buddha and of any other created being who by virtue of asceticism has realised the "body of the Buddha". But just as the temple contains statues and books and encloses a separate world of its own, a *temenos* which represents a sacred area or, like the *maṇḍala*[123], is outwith the non-consecrated world and defended by protective forces — the *chökyongs (c'os skyoṅ)*, "protectors of the Law", on the veranda of a temple which set it apart from all that is profane — so the *chöten* with its eight different types represents the various stages in the life of the Buddha or a series of different spiritual situations. Above all, however, the *chöten* represents the Law which was revealed by the Buddha, as proclaimed by Dinnāga in a celebrated verse, declaring the equivalence of reality, of truth, of the Master's word: it is the *dharmaśarīra*, the "Body of the Law". Buddhism has many formulae which are regarded as containing a synthesis of the Buddha's teaching, and perhaps the most striking of these is a single verse of the Prajñāpāramitā: *ye dharmā hetuprabhavā hetuṃ teṣāṃ, Tathāgataḥ hy avadat teṣāṃ ca yo nirodha evaṃ vādī mahāśramaṇaḥ* ("Of all things that have an origin, of all of them, the Tathāgata, who speaks according to truth, has explained the origin and the end").

To built a *stūpa*, therefore, was to build the body of the Buddha, which was identified with his doctrine; and the better to attain this objective it was the practice, as we have already noted, to deposit in the foundations of a *stūpa* the clay tablets known as *ts'a ts'as* on which were stamped such formulae *(dhāraṇī)* as the one just quoted.

Formulae of this kind, brief statements for mnemonic purposes of sacred texts or invocations, represented a form of *prāṇapratiṣṭhā*, a ceremony which served to convey "life" to a temple, giving it the sacral character which distinguished it from other buildings. In addition it was possible, particularly in western Tibet, to use the window provided for this purpose to deposit in the *chöten* other *ts'a ts'as* — sacred objects, books no longer required for use, damaged paintings or anything else which still possessed a sacred significance.

In a later period the building of *chötens* continued in Tibet for still other purposes. They might be used, for example, for keeping collections of sacred writings — as in the case of the *stūpa* at Gilgit, which provided Sir Aurel Stein, who was present at its demolition, with a rich harvest of manuscripts. In such cases the *chöten* was also the receptacle of the Word, the Law as expressed in the Buddha's revelation: thus the monastery of Sakya, according to a tradition still current which is recorded in the pilgrims' Guide, contains a manuscript collection of the books revealed by the Buddha *(bKa' ạgyur)* in the Uyghur language. *Chötens* also began to be built on the death of a lama who was considered to be particularly holy, the lama's ashes being mixed with earth and used to make *ts'a ts'as* which were then deposited in the *chöten:* a practice which is still found. In some cases *chötens* were brought from distant places: for example the gilded bronze *chöten* in the temple at Ngariṭatsang *(mṄa' ris grwa ts'aṅ)*, of which I shall have more to say later, or those illustrated in *Plate 88,* in a style characteristic of the earliest periods and particularly of the Kadampa *(bKa' gdams pa)* schools which seem to point to Central Asian or Chinese rather than Indian influences.

The *ts'a ts'as* (a word of Prakrit origin) which are so closely associated with the *chötens* are of several different kinds. The commonest are those bearing the various sacred formulae which have been referred to above; others are in the form of a *stūpa* with the verse from the *Prajñāpāramitā* written round it, or may represent a *stūpa*, without inscription, with a conical upper part and a large circular base; and *ts'a ts'as* are also very commonly found representing one or more (usually three) *stūpas* or various divinities, particularly Lokeśvara, Padmapāṇi, Mañjuśrī and Tārā.

We need not consider here the *ts'a ts'as* bearing formulae written in Tibetan, derived from earlier types in Sanskrit characters which were used as a model in Tibet. The many examples of *ts'a ts'as* in my own collection come mainly from *chötens* in western Tibet and Tsang.

It is surprising to note that in Swat, where the Italian archaeological mission has been excavating for some years in a large Buddhist sanctuary, no *ts'a ts'as* have been recovered, although they have been found in Afghanistan and Kashmir. On the eastern side of the Indo-Pakistan peninsula they extend into Burma and Thailand. Almost all the *ts'a ts'as* illustrated in this book bear the formula from the *Prajñāpāramitā* or some other *dhānaṇī* written in the scripts of north-western India or the Ganges valley. Occasionally the inscriptions on the Tibetan *ts'a ts'as* show mistakes in orthography suggesting that the stamps were the work of the first neophytes, poorly versed in Sanskrit. We have very considerable numbers of *ts'a ts'as* with patterns or inscriptions stamped on them, the predominant design being the *stūpa* — either the *stūpa* of the "descent from heaven", which is the commonest *(Plates 84, 89, 90, 93, 94)*, the "*stūpa* of many doors" *(Plates 91, 93, 96, 97)* or the "*stūpa* of Illumination". There are innumerable variants of these types: single *stūpas* or groups of three or more, surmounted by standards waving in the breeze. These clearly refer to particular places of pilgrimage. One appears to represent a group of *stūpas* seen from above *(Plate 95)*. It is interesting to compare *Plate 89* with the *stūpa* at Tholing *(Plate 84)*, in which tradition has it that the remains of the great translator are preserved. Of the divinities of the *Mahāyāna* the one most frequently represented is Lokeśvara or Padmapāṇi, depicted in the *lalitāsana* posture *(Plates 103,*

117

104). The figures are the same as those frequently represented in the rock carvings of Swat, but on *ts'a ts'as* of this kind they are found as far afield as Burma, with some very refined examples in Bengal[124]. The smooth modelling of the specimens discovered in western Tibet may point to influences from the neighbouring countries, but it is difficult to be sure of this in view of the popularity and wide diffusion of the iconographic type.

Other examples showing the Buddha between two Bodhisattvas wearing a diadem, crudely executed works which were no doubt produced by local craftsmen *(Plate 108)*, belong to a school influenced by Kashmiri tradition. There are also representations of purely Tantric divinities[125]. The form of the script makes it possible to date these *ts'a ts'as* to the period between the 10th and 13th centuries. Thereafter the Sanskrit formulae gradually disappear, to be replaced by other formulae in Tibetan *(om maṇi padme hūm, etc.)*; or in some cases there is no inscription of any kind.

Understandably, as the expansion of Buddhism proceeded, as more and more Buddhist pilgrims travelled to India, or when the exodus of Buddhist fugitives from India to Tibet began, the Tibetan communities must have needed larger numbers of stamps for *ts'a ts'as*; but since I have found in some *chötens* examples of various types of *ts'a ts'as*, one or two of which were certainly Indian, we may suppose that some *ts'a ts'as* bought by pilgrims in Indian monasteries were brought into Tibet by their pious owners and deposited in the *chöten* nearest to the pilgrim's temple or village. In any event great significance must be attached to these *ts'a ts'as*, not only because they inaugurated a practice which still survives in Tibet but also because they introduced the Tibetans to iconographic types and models of varied artistic inspiration which blended with other influences, shortly to be discussed, to produce the characteristic achievement of Tibetan art. Thus by continuing and extending the study which I published in 1932 — in which I examined some of the *ts'a ts'as* then available, a very much smaller number than we now have at our disposal — it will become possible to establish, at any rate approximately, what contacts Tibet, and particularly western Tibet and Tsang, had with India and the adjoining countries, including Gilgit and Afghanistan, during the period of the Buddhist revival in Tibet.

Among the most important *chötens* — if we may disregard for the moment the later period — are those founded by the *lotsāva* of Ṭhophu *(K'ro p'u)*, who invited the famous Kashmiri pandit Śākyaśrī to Tibet in the 13th century: for example a *chöten* in the defile between Jonang *(Jo naṅ)* and Shigatse, near a temple in which he had dedicated a statue of Maitreya in 1212. When I visited this building in 1938 it was in a fairly good state of preservation but the paintings in the chapels were badly damaged. Another interesting example is the *chöten* at Gyang *(rGyaṅ) (Plates 78, 79)*, near Lhatse *(Lha rtse)*, which was built with the help of Thangton *(T'aṅ ston)* by the Sakyapa Sonamtashi *(bSod nams bkra šis, 1352–1417)*; the paintings show a distinct Nepalese influence and some reminiscences of Central Asian art, although the work was done almost entirely by Tibetan artists.

The *chöten* at Jonang was built by Sherapgyelthsenpelsangpo *(Šes rab rgyal mts'an dpal bzaṅ po)*, who died in 1360, but was restored in the time of Tāranātha (born 1575). The one at Narthang *(sNar t'aṅ) (Plate 83)* was built by Nyantaksangpopel *(sÑan grags bzaṅ po dpal)*; the one at Gyantse *(Plate 80)*, the largest in Tibet, by the Chögyel *(C'os rgyal)* Raptenkunsangphakpa *(Rab brtan Kun bzaṅ ap'ags pa*, born 1389*)* in the year 1427; the one at Champaling *(Byams pa gliṅ) (Plate 81)* by Thumi Lhuntuptashi *(T'u mi Lhun grub bkra šis)* in 1472.

The "*chötens* of many doors" *(sgo maṅ)* are of particular interest, not only because they are outstanding examples of Tibetan sacred architecture but also because the decoration of their chapels affords valuable evidence on the evolution of Tibetan painting under a variety of artistic influences and on the gradual formation of a uniform style which eventually established its predominance throughout the whole country. The name of this type comes from the fact that it comprised a number of inter-communicating chapels on different levels which allowed the pilgrim to ascend gradually to the *cella* at the top of the whole structure with its figures of the most secret esoteric divinities. The chapels are successively smaller from storey to storey, and their walls are literally covered with paintings representing the various divinities or, most commonly, symbols of esoteric doctrines or pictorial diagrams from the sacred books. The paintings were the work of artists of different schools, which in due time were to play their part in forming the traditional Tibetan style of painting[126].

It is not uncommon to find, near places of particular sanctity, rows of *chötens* built of earth or sun-dried brick; and in such cases it was laid down in certain sacred texts that they should number 108 *(Plate 82)*. The practice of erecting rows of 108 *chötens* is fairly common in western Tibet but rarer in other parts of the country; no doubt it dates from the early days of the revival of Buddhism.

Other *chötens* have an opening right through the base, forming a kind of archway over a road or track, so that wayfarers can pass through underneath. The passage, with its substantial side walls, thus serves as a support for the *chöten* proper. In such cases the ceiling is decorated with paintings of the most popular divinities of the Buddhist pantheon.

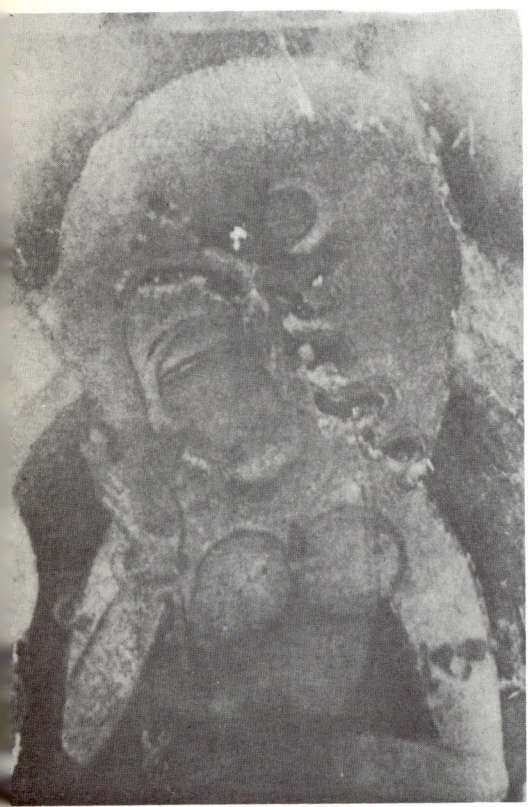

114, 115 ↑ 116 117

119   120

121

122

126

127

128

129

131

132

133, 134 ↑   135   136

137

138

139

140

141

THE GENESIS OF TIBETAN ART

III

The Influence of Neighbouring Countries

Before achieving a style distinctively their own — as they did when they tired of imitating foreign models and their own aesthetic sense, formed by many years of experience, began to find expression — the Tibetans followed the trends which contacts with neighbouring countries had introduced. These influences were exerted in two different ways: either through the presence in Tibet of artists from these other countries (as a result of the attraction which Tibetan Buddhism exerted on Buddhist centres in other countries or of particular historical circumstances — the hostility to Buddhism shown in these countries) or in consequence of the pilgrimages to sacred places in neighbouring countries which were undertaken with increasing frequency by Tibetans.

We have already noted in a previous chapter that at least some of the most important temples in Tibet built between the dynastic period and the revival of Buddhism in the 10th and 11th centuries showed the influence of foreign artistic trends or contained works of art belonging to schools which were manifestly not Tibetan[127]. The Tibetans themselves recognise that their art, whether painting or sculpture, originally depended on foreign models or derived from them, and are very ready to admit that among the most valuable treasures in their temples are numerous works by foreign artists. The written Guides to the monasteries, as we have seen, draw particular attention to these works, hallowed as they are by ancient traditions which in most cases have some foundation in historical fact. But although the Tibetan authorities on Indian or Central Asian or Chinese art describe these particular works they are not, of course, sufficiently knowledgeable to recognise other works of equal or greater importance. Thus if we consider only the Guide of mK'yen brtse[128] we learn that a statue of Gonpo *(mGon po)* was brought to Sakya by the *lotsāva* of Nyen *(gÑan)*[129]; but the same monastery has as one of its most precious possessions a conch with a lid of wrought silver, said to have been a present from an Indian king to a Chinese ruler and later given by Khubilai to the monastery of Sakya, the abbots of which, from Phakpa *(aP'ags pa)* onwards, had become his teachers[130]. Similarly the representation of Ḍölma *(sGrol ma)* in the Ḍölma-lhakhang *(sGrol ma lha k'aṅ)* in the same monastery is said to have been found in some unknown spot and presented to the monastery by the *lotsāva* of Ba ri. The Mañjuśrī known as Ziöbarva *(gZi 'od ạbar ba)* which is also worshipped in Sakya monastery is of Kashmiri origin and is said to have been a gift from Sakyapenchen *(Sa skya Paṇ c'en)*[131]. We shall have more to say about this later.

The statue of Maitreya at Gadong *(dGa' sdoṅ)* is also of Indian origin[132], having been brought from eastern India by Tshulṭhimchungne *(Ts'ul k'rims ạbyuṅ gnas)*. The principal statue at Zhalu *(Ža lu)*, representing Khasarpana, was brought to the monastery by Sherapchungne *(Šer rab ạbyuṅ gnas)*, who had obtained it at Bodhgayā.

At Samye pilgrims are shown a statue belonging to Padmavajra[133]. The gilded bronze statue of Avalokiteśvara in the Potala is believed to have been brought from Nepal by Ākaramati. Lhasa, as we have already seen [134], was famous for two different statues from China or India: the Jobo Mikyödorje *(Mi bskyod rdo rje)*, Akṣobhyavajra, presented by the Nepalese wife of Songtsengampo, is believed to be work of Viśvakarman, the artist of the gods, and the statue of Ḍölma *(Dar len ma)* now in the Ṭhulnang is said to have been a gift from the same queen, like the Maitreya Chökorma *(C'os kor ma)*. The statue of Avalokiteśvara with eleven heads enjoys the epithet *rangchung (raṅ byuṅ)*, "self-created", since legend has it that it was commissioned from a Nepalese artist who later confessed that it was not the work of his hands but had arisen spontaneously in front of him. According to Putön[135], however, it was an import into Tibet from Nepal.

Confirmation of these facts is provided by certain Tibetan writers who, basing themselves on Indian traditions, refer to various foreign influences and indeed mention the names of the leaders of particular artistic schools in the peninsula from which certain Tibetan artistic trends were derived, as well as by the authors of treatises who, while chiefly concerned with the various methods of casting and modelling statues, give some brief preliminary indications about the predominant styles in Tibet and the origin of these styles. These statements by Tibetan writers do not rest only on the observation of works of art still to be seen in temples: they are also based, as we have noted, on an Indian source recorded by the famous polygraph Tāranātha[136] and one of his successors, Sumpakhenpo *(Sum pa mk'an po)*[137], who used the same source.

The prototypes and the first masters of Tibetan art would thus go back to the school of Dhīmān and his son Bitpala *(Vidyāpāla?)* who lived in the time of Devapāla and Dharmapāla (8th–9th century) and are believed to have worked at Nālandā. Dhīmān's influence is said to have made itself felt in eastern India (i.e. Bengal) and his son's in central India, extending from there into the western provinces and Nepal. Sumpakhenpo adds the very important piece of information that there were also a number of other flourishing artistic schools: one in Kashmir, centred on Hasarāja, and another in southern India to which the leading artists of the area — Jaya, Vijaya and Parojaya — were at least indirectly attached. This evidence is important because, as we shall see, there are paintings at Phüntshokling which show analogies with the art of southern India.

This source speaks of *zobas (bzo ba)*, artists or craftsmen who were masters of the two branches of art in question: the casting of statues and "drawing" *(lha bris, ri mo)*, i.e. painting. It is clear at any rate that the schools of which they were the leading exponents were represented in Tibet, whether this was the result of direct contact or of transmission through Kashmiri or

Nepalese intermediaries. To this must be added the Hindu Shāhī influence which can readily be detected in a number of statues I have seen in Tibetan monasteries and certain earlier influences from Nepal or Chinese Central Asia (Khotan) which are referred to, for example, in the Khatangdenga *(bKa' t'aṅ sde lṅa)*.

The information recorded in an early Tibetan chronicle[138], even allowing for later alterations, is of particular importance. According to this source, artists were invited to Tibet from China, Khotan, Nepal and Kashmir in the reign of King Ṭhitsukdetsen *(K'ri gtsug lde brtsan)*; and we are told that the king particularly admired the work of an artist from Khotan, known as the "king of the style of Khotan", who worked in Tibet along with his three sons and stone-carvers from Nepal. The chronicles of the fifth Dalai Lama also refer to the presence of artists from these countries[139]; and there is further evidence of Khotanese and Indian influence in the Iwang inscriptions already discussed[140].

Before the ravages of war from which so many monasteries suffered during the intestine struggles which rent Tibet for several centuries and the fires which wrought havoc in many places works of this kind must have been much more numerous than they are today. Another factor which has caused the loss of many paintings is the Tibetans' zeal for restoration, which takes a rather different form from restoration as normally conceived in the West: when the frescoes on the walls of temples began to show signs of dilapidation the practice was to erase them completely and paint new ones in their place.

It is established, therefore, both by the evidence of the written sources and by the traditions which still survive in the monasteries, that the birth of Tibetan art is to be attributed to foreign influences and models. Four main sources can be identified — Nepal, China, Central Asia and India. In India anumber of sub-groups can be distinguished — central India, eastern India, southern India, western India, and of course Nepal. In China the sources talk of an older style and a modern style. The school of sculpture which came into fashion in the time of the Chögyels *(C'os rgyal)* — the kings — is divided by the same sources into an early, an intermediate and a late period; and they mention also the artistic trends brought in by the Uyghurs[141]. The schools of western India showed close affinities with those of Kashmir, while, according to a celebrated Tibetan polygraph, Pemakarpo *(Pad ma dkar po)*, the schools of the dynastic period showed influences from Li (Khotan) [142].

Foreign Works and Local Imitations

Apart from the distinction of styles, which is necessarily vague and often arbitrary, the authors who have concerned themselves with this subject also take account of the different materials used and the quality of workmanship. The views they have expressed are confirmed by the large number of non-Tibetan paintings and pieces of sculpture to be seen in Tibetan monasteries and by the evident imitation of foreign models, bearing witness to the variety of artistic trends which existed side by side in Tibet. This evidence demonstrates the validity of the suggestion already made that certain works were imported or reflected the arrival in Tibet of foreign painters who attracted large numbers of pupils and taught them to paint, to cast statues or to carve wood. The memory of some of these schools still survives in western Tibet: for example Luk, now a mere village of a few mean houses, was regarded as one of the country's leading artistic centres.

Plate 155 shows a statue found at Luk, formerly in the small local temple and traditionally attributed to an artist who once lived here. In a later period Tanak *(rTa nag)* became one of the leading centres, while eastern Tibet remained under Chinese influence.

It is unnecessary to repeat here what has already been said in our discussion of the temples, but it may be worth recalling that very little evidence survives from the early period, the time of the kings — at any rate from the reign of Ṭhisongdetsen onwards. The bells to be seen at Samye, Ṭhantuk *(K'ra ạbrug)* and Yerpa follow Chinese models and may have been made by Chinese craftsmen living in Tibet, for the inscriptions are in Tibetan. In the monastery of Ngariṭatsang is a *chöten* which certainly dates from the T'ang period *(Plate 87)* and may have been imported from Central Asia[143]. Also from Central Asia is a *thangka* (painting on cloth) showing a number of Bodhisattvas, each with his name written in Chinese characters; unfortunately my photograph of this item is so poor as to be unsuitable for reproduction.

For the reasons already indicated, it is difficult to make any confident statement about the Jokhang in Lhasa. Only the most skilful restoration will reveal whether any part of this temple dates back to the time of the kings. The pillars round the atrium appear to me to be much later than the period of foundation, and suggest a comparison with the corresponding features at Samada *(Plate 126)*. The older parts of the temple must be dated to its rebuilding at the time of the reintroduction of Buddhism.

With the re-establishment of Buddhism our material begins to be abundant. I have already mentioned the wall paintings at Mangnang *(Maṅ naṅ)* in western Tibet, which establish beyond all doubt the presence of Kashmiri painters in this area. There are also frescoes at Tholing and Tsaparang depicting various episodes in the life of the Buddha; *Plate 104* shows one of these, the Buddha taking his first steps. But painters were not the only artists now practising in Tibet. Rinchensangpo also brought in sculptors and perhaps casters of statues — although many statues were probably imported from outside the country. According to one of his biographers, Rinchensangpo commissioned a bronze statue of his father from a Kashmiri artist named Bhitaka *(Bi ta ka?)*. This information is important from two points of view: first because it confirms once again the part played by Kashmir in the formation of Tibetan art, and also because it points to a funerary custom practised by the Mongols but attested in Tibet only by the royal tombs[144]. The flow of foreign works into Tibet must have grown as the influence of Islam spread and the Buddhist communities in Afghanistan and Central Asia were eliminated, their surviving members being driven to seek refuge elsewhere.

I have already referred to the fragments of wood from the doorways of the temples at Tabo, Tsaparang and Alchi *(Plates 129, 136)*: their connection with the art of Kashmir is not in doubt[145].

Similarly there is no uncertainty about the attribution to Kashmiri sculptors of the doorway at Tsaparang *(Plates 133, 138)*, with panels depicting various episodes from the life of the Buddha. Among other works with the same origin are some sculpture in wood from Alchi *(Plates 134, 135, 139, 150)* and a statue in wood from Luk *(Plate 144)*, a site to which we have frequently had occasion to refer. Kashmiri artists were also responsible for the doorway of the small temple at Lhatse dedicated to the Kashmiri teacher Gayādhara *(Plate 137)*. These last works are of particular interest for their use of a motif commonly found in Indian sculpture, the two river goddesses who symbolise the Yamunā and the Gaṅgā. Also of Kashmiri origin is a fragment of a gilded bronze nimbus from Chang with the figure of a monk holding a jar for alms[146]. At Kojarnāth, near the frontier of Nepal, there are some magnificent pieces of sculpture in wood[147]; the principal statue, which draws a continual flow of pilgrims (and which I was able to photograph only after I had succeeded, with great difficulty, in securing the removal of the cloth which covered it) is Indian work, probably from Nālandā[148]. The statue of Vajrapāṇi at Tholing *(Plate 127)* is from Kashmir. At the monastery of Iwang, where the adoption of two different styles, the Indian and the Khotanese[149], is attested by inscriptions, the standing figures of Bodhisattvas with the ends of their cloaks turned outwards are very similar to their counterparts in the temples of Central Asia. Another distinctive feature in these figures is the nimbus, which rises to a point above the head: a type found at Kulu and Bajaurā[150] and elsewhere throughout the Himalayan provinces, for example in Chambā and Spiti *(Plate 142)*, where there were artistic schools of great interest and originality. In the temples at Iwang and Samada, on the other hand, the form of the nimbuses, often with a curving lower part, the rhythmic pattern of folds in the bell-shaped cloaks and the pictorial effects confirm the evidence of the inscriptions and suggest either contacts with Central Asia or some influence transmitted from that region[151].

Still more significant in this respect is another chapel in which the standing figures of Bodhisattvas are richly clad in long draperies decorated with relief medallions containing lions, birds and floral motifs which show clear Sassanid influence[152]. This is not an isolated example, for similar garments, also clearly of Sassanid origin, are found at Nesar and in chapels at Chasa *(Bya sa)* and Ḍanang *(Plates 162, 163)*, to the south of the Tsangpo. This indicates that the fashion for Sassanid dress, or for garments modelled on Sassanid types, had a long life in Tibet: it may well have been adopted in the first place by the nobles and then transferred to the figures of Bodhisattvas, commonly called *rgyal sras* or "kings' sons"[153]. We do not know exactly when these temples were built, but if Iwang corresponds to Yemar *(g Ye dmar)* in the *Myaṅ c'uṅ* (a manuscript chronicle of Gyantse) its presumed founder was Lharjechöchang *(Lha rje c'os byaṅ)*, an earlier incarnation of Śākyaśrī, who arrived in Tibet in 1204. This would put Lharjechöchang's arrival earlier than that date, but it is not possible to be any more definite than that.

143

145, 146 147

153
154

157 ↑ 158 159

161 ↑   162   163

164,165

167, 168, 169

170

171

172

175

176

177   178   179

180

181

182

183

184

185

186, 187, 188 ↑

190, 191

192, 193

194 ↑   195   196

197, 198 ↑   199   200

To these examples, which give firm if indirect evidence of Sassanid influence, we must add the silver (or silver-plated) cup published by Snellgrove and Richardson[154], which shows a series of figures alternating with highly stylised leafless trees, in a manner suggesting Hellenistic influence, while the base, decorated with waves and fishes, follows Chinese traditions which can, however, also be seen on other Sassanid cups.

To illustrate the extraordinary number of Indian statues in Tibet we may consider, for example, the Sakyapa temple of Zhithok *(bŽi t'og)*, which has hundreds of such statues set out on long shelves or ledges in the veranda at the top of the temple. Not all of these are Buddhist — they include a Jain statue of the 13th or 14th century *(Plates 157, 158)*[155]. In total they constitute the largest collection known to me of Indian statues in the Hindu Shāhī, Kashmiri, Pāla and Sena styles *(Plates 145, 147, 151-153)*. Some of them are certainly imports from Nālandā, Kurkihar and Bengal *(Plate 166)*.

In addition to statues — either works in bronze or of the type known as *aṣṭadhātu*, made of eight different metals, which were regarded as particularly precious — the pilgrims brought with them the paintings known as *paṭas* in Sanskrit and *thangkas (t'aṅ ka)* in Tibetan. Although these are now hung in temples their name indicates that they were rolled up and carried by travellers — as they still are today — to provide protection from evil spirits, or were used by minstrels to illustrate the episodes they were describing. In the absence of the originals on which they were modelled it is difficult to be sure which were the predominant styles; but on geographical grounds and on the basis of comparison with the works of sculpture which have come down to us it is possible to say that the Kashmiri style at first predominated in western Tibet, to be followed later by the Nepalese style.

The Kashmiri and Nepalese Styles

Departing from the view I expressed in an earlier work[156], I am now inclined to believe that the nimbus of a statue venerated at Narthang is of Kashmiri origin and not derived from a Bengali model *(Plate 140)*. This represents, with a dignity of execution which has rarely been equalled, a series of episodes from the life of the Buddha, surrounded by scrollwork. It is remarkable for the delicacy of its workmanship, which is much superior to that of the doorways at Tholing and Tsaparang. It is part of the nimbus illustrated in Lin I-ssu's *Hsi-ts'ang fu chiao i shu*[157], which dates it to the year 1093 (Sung period). I do not know what evidence there is for this dating, since I was unable to see any inscription when I visited Narthang. The connection with Kashmir, however, is demonstrated by the style of the work and also by comparison with a statue, perhaps dating from an earlier period *(Plate 172)*, which is reproduced by Pal[158] — although it is difficult to establish any exact relationship between a statue and a nimbus, since the former may have been adapted to the latter in a later period. In the same monastery is a statue of uncertain origin which is reproduced in *Plate 176*; nor am I able to identify the origin of the other statue illustrated in *Plate 161*, which is certainly not Tibetan. With these works must also be associated the nimbus in the monastery of Nanying *(gNas rñiṅ)* illustrated in *Plate 141*[159].

The two statuettes of Tārā at Nyethang, said to have been brought from India by Atīśa *(Plate 175)*, are certainly not Nepalese but must have been produced in Tibet at a much later period.

Probably also of Kashmiri origin is the silver mounting of a shell in the monastery of Pökhang *(sPos k'aṅ)*, which was founded by a disciple of the Khache Penchen *(K'a c'e Paṅ c'en,* Śākyaśrī*) (Plate 165)*. At Samye only a few examples of Indian work have survived, the others having perished in the ravages of destruction and fire: mention should, however, be made of a bronze statue, to be compared with the figures of Tārā, which come from Tripura *(Plate 147)*[160]. Some of these statues are of gilded bronze, but most of them are in a very dark bronze such as is found in Bengal and Gangetic India, also during the Pāla and Sena periods; others are in the alloy of eight metals *(aṣṭadhātu)* which was regarded in India as particularly precious[161].

A work of particular interest is the figure of Padmapāṇi from Pökhang *(sPos k'aṅ)* which is reproduced in *Plate 160*. Although the features and the hair style show strong affinities with southern Indian work, the statue may nevertheless come from Bengal, where numerous examples of figures with slightly elongated, almost ovoid, faces can be found[162]. Mention should also be made of a type of bronze lamp with lotus leaves which open and close, containing the coupled figures, in high relief, of the male and female divinities, *yab yum*[163].

Similar conclusions may be drawn from the many *chötens* to be found inside temples. Since they are frequently made from sheets of bronze covering an inner structure, it is not certain that these *chötens*, which are undoubtedly of non-Tibetan origin, were brought in ready made from somewhere outside the country. The separate pieces may have been assembled on the spot, and some of the pieces may have been made in Tibet by foreign craftsmen, particularly in western Tibet but also in the central region. There are some magnificent examples of Kashmiri origin, including some with motifs derived from Central Asia *(Plate 171)*; in their decoration and workmanship they are very similar to the nimbuses which have been discussed on an earlier page. Gradually, however, for a variety of reasons, the predominance passed to the Nepalese schools. The decline of the great Buddhist centres in India interrupted the intensive and continuous exchanges between the two countries which were maintained until about the time of Atīśa; and the proximity of Nepal, the increasingly frequent trading contacts with that country and the thriving state of Buddhism there — all these factors combined meant that the interests of the Tibetan community now converged on Kathmandu and the neighbouring regions. The Kashmiri work we have been considering now gave place to statues and *chötens* produced by Nepalese artists and craftsmen. Among the *chötens*, however, we can point to a single exception: the fine example to be seen in the monastery at Narthang, a work of outstanding quality which clearly comes from South-East Asia *(Plate 169)*. It is difficult to explain how it reached Narthang, no doubt after an intermediate halt somewhere in India. Two other bronze *chötens* also deserve attention: in one of them *(Plate 167)* the figures of lions point to a cultural area connected with Iran, while the other *(Plate 168)* has a curious pattern of squares which shows affinities with Islamic and particularly Ghaznavid art, recalling for example the decoration of the doors in Mahmud's mausoleum at Ghaznī.

Before fusing into the expression of a purely Tibetan style, the same variety of influences can be identified in the nimbuses round the heads of the statues *(Plates 173, 174)*. In one type, some of the best examples of which come from Kashmir, the figures of Buddha or of Bodhisattvas are enclosed in a frame of circles or scrollwork; in others the figural representation gives place to floral motifs in high relief, often elaborated into baroque arabesques — reflecting a popular Nepalese style which is not easily distinguished from Tibetan art in the proper sense. These nimbuses are remarkable both for their number and their variety — indicating that at the time of the Buddhist diaspora Tibet offered a safe refuge to which manuscripts and works of art were sent for preservation.

What we have said about sculpture applies equally to painting. Reference has already been made to the paintings at Mangnang, and also to the *thangkas*[164] which were undoubtedly painted by Kashmiri artists, although they often show traces of influences from Central Asia[165].

The miniatures in the manuscripts of the *Prajñāpāramitā* date from the 11th and 12th centuries. We can see, however, how in the course of time, lacking the direct influence of the master, the artist's manner becomes more languid, the decorative elements predominate and the chiaroscuro effects are toned down *(Plates 148, 149)*. Nevertheless the garments of the offering-bearers still have something reminiscent of Central Asia[166].

It is evident at any rate that the Mangnang paintings are not an isolated phenomenon: in addition to the miniatures in the manuscripts of the *Prajñāpāramitā* we can adduce the school, also of Kashmiri origin, which is represented at Alchi. At this monastery, however, at least three periods can be identified. The first of these appears to be contemporary with Rinchensangpo[167] and some illuminated manuscripts at Tholing; they are certainly not by the same artists but they reflect the same traditions and the same artistic manner. This school was now worn out and in decline, as can be clearly seen in a painting from the life of the Buddha[168].

In the second period we find a new manner, which can be dated to the 14th century, perhaps to the time of Prince Riñcana Bhoṭṭa of Ladakh *(rgyal bu Rin c'en)*, who seized power in Kashmir and reigned there for three years. To this period can be attributed a painting of two Tibetan women offering refreshment to a king or high dignitary wearing a kaftan of Iranian type (decorated with golden lions enclosed in circles)[169]. I believe that these frescoes are the work of Tibetan painters established in Kashmir, since a similar decoration is found at Gyang, perhaps following Central Asian models (cf. the paintings at Pendzhikent and Balalyk Tepe). The third period is represented by frescoes in which the influence of the illuminations in Moghul manuscripts is very evident. This marks the end of the school which produced the paintings at Mangnang and the earliest work at Alchi and the beginning of a new and predominantly Islamic style[170].

This Central Asian influence, which we have already observed in some of the sculpture from Iwang, is still quite perceptible in some paintings from Gyang *(Plate 123)*[171]. It is now, however, no more than the last distant echo of a dying tradition.

One picture *(Plate 183)* is of particular interest. Although it shows a group of emissaries bringing tribute (which might suggest that the painter was concerned to depict in a fairly realistic way an event that had actually taken place) the workmanship is quite un-Tibetan — as can be seen, for example, in the manner of representing the horses.

The influence of the earliest Nepalese manner, with which we are familiar in the numerous manuscripts decorated with miniatures in the principal Tibetan monasteries *(Plates 148, 149)*, can be seen in a very fine *thangka*[172] which has counterparts in Nepalese manuscripts of the 10th and 11th centuries; and we find it again at Nesar[173] and Iwang[174]. In any study of the history and development of Nepalese painting the frescoes in the large *"chötens* of many doors" provide evidence of the culmination and fusion together of the most varied traditions; there are even some small paintings which offer striking similarities to the paintings at Qyzil. In seeking to establish the separate elements which went into the creation of this painting we cannot confine ourselves to the influences which have already been discussed and to Kashmir, Khotan and Nepal: the whole of Central Asia, extending as far afield as Turfan, Tumchuq, Qyzil and Bäzälik, may have played a part in their development, working through channels and in ways which we are now unable to identify; and this influence may have survived in particular isolated schools for a very long period.

Another centre, roughly half way between Kashmir and Central Asia, may have been Gilgit[175], which long maintained contacts with Tibet, continuing until the 14th century to send teachers and Bonpo sorcerers into the country. We have two wooden book covers from Gilgit which bear witness to the existence in that region of particular artistic trends which, in the absence of other evidence, we cannot define more closely. The paintings at Gyang, in a distinctive style which bears no relationship to the artistic schools in Tibet which we know best, may well reflect influences coming from Qyzil in a late stage of its development. And it may be significant that the wall paintings at Jonang *(Plate 184)* are divided into squares, each containing a particular scene, in the same way as at Qyzil[176].

The small circles round the head of a figure *(Plate 186)* are a clear reminiscence of the bead necklaces worn by personages of high rank — kings, donors, etc. — in Central Asian paintings, at Qyzil and Bäzälik. The manner of representing horses also points in the same direction[177], to Chotsho and even to Pendzhikent[178], although the Central Asian work shows a much higher degree of skill. On the other hand there are certain scenes in which the composition, the dress of the figures and the manner of painting trees and women gathering flowers continue the pictorial traditions of India[179].

Nepalese influence continued to make itself felt for centuries, and we know on the basis of exact evidence, for example, that Kungasangpo *(Kun dga' bzaṅ po)*[180] caused the monastery of Ngor *(Ṅor)*, built in 1429, to be decorated by Nepalese artists.

This Nepalese influence on Tibetan painting was felt not only in the wall frescoes and the *thangkas* painted by Nepalese artists who had been brought to Tibet for the purpose but also in the continual commissioning of work by the Tibetan monasteries and their direct acquisitions of illuminated manuscripts. There are large numbers of richly illuminated manuscripts at Sakya and Ngor; and as a rule these works possess the great advantage of being dated.

Mention must also be made of the fabrics which were regularly imported to meet the needs of great personages and high ecclesiastical dignitaries, who used them to embellish the temples or to frame *thangkas*. I have seen many such fabrics, but it is possible to illustrate only two examples: a fragment of Chinese material, probably of the Yüan period, depicting a procession of women *(Plate 180)* and a Nepalese hanging from Narthang representing a large *stūpa*, perhaps Svayambhūnāth *(Plate 181)*. Some of the scenes depicted on the former are reminiscent of the frescoes at Narthang *(Plate 191)*.

Nor must the student of Tibetan art neglect such objects of everyday use as lamps and censers. The finest example of such work which I have seen was an inlaid censer of the Sakyapa period, apparently from the eastern provinces of Tibet, representing a tradition of craftsmanship which is still alive today.

Towards a Tibetan Koine

The development of Tibetan art follows a similar course to that of literature: first the bringing together of original works, then the production of faithful translations, then the commentaries, and finally the summaries and syntheses — all within the unique and indissoluble tradition of Buddhism, through the work of the various schools and particular sects which branched off from it. Just as the process of systematising the dogma ended

204

205

with Tsongkhapa (1357–1419) — each school having by then acquired its distinctive characteristics — so in the 14th and 15th centuries the *concordia discors* of the different artistic trends was brought to an end. Many of these trends had made themselves felt in Tibet; models of different kinds were to be found throughout the country; and teachers of many different schools had worked there. In the time of the Sakyapa and of Putön there began the systematisation of dogma and the Tantric liturgy which, by translating the esoteric theories of the schools into pictorial symbols — a process in which Putön played a decisive part — exerted considerable influence on the figural representation of the ritual and meditative dogma of the Tantras. The result was that when the principal monasteries grew in power and authority the different artistic schools gradually blended their various traditions into a more uniform expression; and the new forms which emerged from this fusion progressively broke free from the earlier traditions and continued to develop on their own. The building of the large "*chötens* of many doors" or *kubums* was a development of great importance in the creation of this artistic *koine*, which falls outside the scope of this survey of the archaeology and ancient art of Tibet. This was the climax and, in a sense, the final dying out of the varied artistic traditions which had flourished in Tibet: the memory of these traditions was forgotten, and soon all trace of them was lost. Tibetan art now took on its definitive form, the form in which we know it today, and never thereafter departed from the established tradition. New political situations might occasionally give rise to particular artistic developments, but these were limited to the monastery or monasteries concerned. This was the case, for example, at Zhalu *(Ža lu)*, built in the style of the Yüan dynasty of China, with majolicas and arabesques and a gigantic statue of the Buddha in which Chinese influence is evident *(Plates 72, 73)*. We know that Chinese and Mongol artists did in fact work there: in this respect Zhalu was an isolated case which, so far as can be established, had no wider influence. *Plate 111* shows a perfume brazier of the Yüan period from this monastery.

Artists trained in the Chinese tradition also worked on the decoration of the *kubum* at Narthang: in the paintings in the interior of the temple the architecture is Chinese, the processions depicted are Chinese, and some of the scenes *(Plates 191)* are also typically Chinese. This is, however, an exceptional instance; and similarly Phüntshokling, redecorated by Tāranātha (born 1575), is absolutely unique. The frescoes at Phüntshokling have no connection with the Tibetan tradition: Tāranātha had frequent contacts with India, he welcomed Indian teachers like Buddhagupta, and no doubt he brought in Indian artists to decorate his temple. These artists belonged to different schools which are difficult to define accurately, but there is a hint in their work of certain features characteristic of southern India. In interpreting after their own fashion the subjects selected by Tāranātha they show a remarkable power of expression, with a lively sense of movement which is exemplified particularly in their pictures of galloping horses, great virtuosity in the use of contrasting colours, and notable skill in depicting the graceful flowing lines of women's bodies *(Plates 192–196)*.

It is important to remember that eastern Tibet always remained under the predominant influence of China; and through the intermediary of the monasteries this influence was superimposed on the Tibetan *koine* or blended with it. This is particularly evident in certain iconographic types which have their prototype in China, for example the cycle of the sixteen or eighteen Arhats or the four Lokapālas; Vaiśravaṇa in particular retained his iconography of Central Asian origin *(Plate 189)*. As time went on, however, these variations tended to disappear, absorbed into a common language which admitted only the occasional Nepalese or Chinese feature, depending on the fashion of the day. Then from the 13th and 14th centuries onwards the long cherished store of works of art brought in from outside Tibet, venerated as a precious legacy from the country which had given Buddhism its spiritual, philosophical and religious culture, the vast accumulation of imported statues, paintings and *chötens* by foreign artists and craftsmen of all periods which makes the great monasteries such a treasure-house of art, began to exert an active and stimulating influence on Tibetan art; and having once found its distinctive manner, that art never thereafter abandoned it, save on a few rare and fleeting occasions.

Stone Sculpture

Although there is certainly no shortage of stone in Tibet, and we have references in our sources to certain statues carved from a type of stone which may be alabaster, stone figures carved in the round have always been extremely rare. The reason may be that numbers of original works in bronze, copper or other metals, which were lighter to carry, had been brought in by pilgrims, while there were no pieces of stone sculpture available to provide models. The sources do, however, indicate that a stone statue of Songtsengampo was erected over his tomb, and that the statues of the three Protectors *(rigs gsum mgon po)* and the five Buddhas *(rgyal ba rigs lṅa)* in the temple at Ṭhantuk *(K'ra ạbrug)*, traditionally dated to the reign of Songtsengampo, were also of stone. That the craft of stone-carving was in fact practised in Tibet is proved by the reference in the *sBa bzhed* to the artists, or rather sculptors, whom Ṭhitsukdetsen *(K'ri gtsug lde brtsan)* brought from Nepal and by the stone figure of a lion published by H.E. Richardson *(Plate 47)*[181]. The statue came from the tomb of Repachen, which was certainly imitated from Chinese models. We also have a carved tortoise from a funerary tumulus (reminiscent of the tomb of Hsiao-hsin, who died in 518), also showing Chinese inspiration. In addition, as Richardson notes and as I have myself observed, there is a stone tortoise in the courtyard of the west temple at Samye, set under a gargoyle in the form of a dragon's jaws. The tortoise, which must have been brought from some other building and may originally have been the base of a statue or pillar, is in the Chinese style of the T'ang period.

The case of the *dorings* which have already been discussed is of course different. These have ornamental motifs which no doubt had some symbolic significance[182]. The pillars themselves were frequently topped by a small pagoda-type roof with inward-curving corners, in the Chinese manner. As a rule there is a spherical or near-spherical ball at the tip of the roof; or alternatively the roof *(žol rdo riṅ)* is surmounted by a pyramid, also of stone, on top of which is another stone in the shape of a large pine-cone.

Figures carved from the native rock are often found on the path leading to a holy place, at fords or other perilous places, near suspension bridges or at places where there is a danger of landslides. The oldest of these represent the Buddha; the later ones are of other divinities who were credited with the power to protect the faithful, in particular Avalokiteśvara and Tārā. We may think, for example, of the rock carving near Phaongkha *(P'a boṅ ka)*, where tradition had it that a statue of Khasarpana was set up in the time of Songtsengampo; and there are others near Chushul *(C'u šul)* and Marpori *(dMar po ri) (Plates 199, 200)*[183]. There also are rock sculptures of the same type near Lhasa; in the absence of inscriptions or other evidence it is difficult to date them, but they appear to be very old *(Plate 199)*.

I believe that this practice was introduced into Tibet mainly in imitation of the north-western provinces of the Indian peninsula, particularly Swat (Uḍḍiyāna), where the conditions are similar and travel equally difficult. The tracks followed by pilgrims were all signposted by rock carvings which had both a sacred and a functional purpose[184]. The two carvings reproduced *(Plates 199, 200)* show striking analogies to those found in Swat, which from the time of Padmasaṃbhava onwards maintained relationships with Tibet, traded with it by way of Gilgit and Ladakh, and was always regarded by the Tibetans as a holy land.

There are also works of sculpture in sun-baked earth and plaster *(Plates 198, 201)* which show considerable artistic skill. Their dating is, however, very uncertain unless we know the date of the monastery to which they belonged. The figure illustrated in *Plate 201* shows some trace of Chinese influence.

CONCLUSION

Clearly it was necessary for Tibet to reach a sufficient degree of political unity before it could achieve an aesthetic conception of its own enabling it to express its particular sensibility, developed from the various models which had been offered for its imitation and the various artistic schools which had been brought into the country by small groups of refugees from Central Asia, India and elsewhere as a result of historical circumstances. This conception was slow to emerge, for each monastic community was a separate unit which had its own particular links or associations with one or other centre of culture. Nor must we forget that the Tibetans' devout acceptance of Buddhism and their reluctance, as enthusiastic neophytes, to tamper in any way with the iconographic schemes which were held to be unalterable as having been devised by the Buddha himself, imposed limits which the artists could not ignore. The figures were drawn in accordance with the standards laid down in a rigorous body of doctrine brought in from India, with only restricted scope for the occasional minor variations; the colours to be used were specified in the liturgy; and the great *maṇḍalas* which translated into the language of line and colour particular moments in the process of meditation could not depart from the subtle injunctions of Tantric soteriology without losing their spiritual efficacy.

The artist was thus unable to give free range to his imagination, except when these hieratic and mystical schemes included biographical details — events from the life of the Buddha or the Bodhisattvas, descriptions of the various paradises or stories of the lives of saints, who were frequently abbots of the great monasteries. It is only then that a breath of life appears in the paintings and the element of contrast between the doctrinal message of a painting and the artist's freedom from the usual constraints allows him to indulge his fancy to the full.

Thus if we want to obtain any valid idea of the development of Tibetan art the urgent requirement, as soon as circumstances permit, is to identify and record all those external influences which transmitted new impulses to the Tibetans and led them to find in sacred art the essential principle of their unity. Secular art and craftsmanship, on the other hand, remained largely under Chinese influence or perpetuated atypical local forms.

One final point may be noted. The figures of donors which are commonly found in Indian statuary, whether stone or metal, in all artistic periods, as well as in Hindu Shāhī art and in the art of Kashmir, Gangetic India and Bengal, and are still depicted, though rather less frequently, in Nepalese art down to our own day, are almost completely absent from Tibetan art. They occur, if at all, on certain *thangkas*, and then always under the influence of Nepal.

We thus observe once again that the archaeology and indeed the whole history of Tibetan art are not yet a body of established fact but a programme of research for the future. In this study the central point to remember is that Tibet is not an island cut off from the rest of the world but a meeting place of different cultures, an area in which India, the Himalayan regions, China, Iran and Central Asia all exert their various influences. Further light on these questions can only come — and we must hope that its coming will not be too long delayed — from painstaking investigation of Tibetan archaeology and careful study of the development of Tibetan art; and the solution to problems of such evident complexity will clearly demand a very extensive acquaintance with the different cultures of Asia. Accordingly the most urgent tasks facing Chinese archaeologists are to compile a complete inventory of all the extant material, both archaeological and artistic, in the province of Tibet; to ensure that it is recorded and photographed; and to undertake excavations on the most important sites, including in particular cemeteries, royal tombs and other sites of special significance in the Yarlung valley and the area round Lhasa.

NOTES

(References in the form "Pelliot, 1961" are to items listed in the Bibliography).

[1] I am grateful to the Istituto Poligrafico dello Stato, Rome, for allowing me to reproduce a number of illustrations from my *Tibetan Painted Scrolls* (Tucci, 1949), to my friend H.E. Richardson for sending me some of his own photographs, to the Museum of Oriental Art in Rome for the reproductions of a number of *thangkas* from the museum and to Professor L. Petech for kindly revising the final proofs.

[2] Tucci, 1932–41.

[3] Tucci, 1949.

[4] *K'ao ku*, 1972, No. 1.

[5] Pelliot, 1961, pp. 80–81.

[6] "Eisenschmiede und Dämonen in Indien", *Internationales Archiv fur Ethnographie*, vol. 37, Suppl., Leiden, 1939.

[7] "Der göttliche Schmied in Tibet", *Folklore Studies*, 19, 1960, 263.

[8] Heine-Geldern, 1951.

[9] Cf., however, Rudenko, 1969, Plate XXI, No. 5.

[10] Bunker, etc., 1970, Plates 85 and 86.

[11] On the significance of the mountain in Tibet, see Stein, 1972, pp. 202 ff., and Tucci, 1970, pp. 187 and 241.

[12] Tucci, 1970, p. 241.

[13] Bunker, etc., 1970, Plate 112.

[14] Tucci, 1970, p. 240.

[15] Hambis, 1954, pp. 483 ff. and Plates LIX–LXIV.

[16] Rudenko, 1969, Plate XXI, Nos. 3 and 4.

[17] Rudenko, 1969, Plate XXI, Nos. 5 and 7.

[18] Dauvillier, 1948 and 1950.

[19] Hambis, 1954, pp. 483 ff.

[20] Seligman and Beck, "Far Eastern Glass: Some Western Origins", in *Museum of Far Eastern Antiquities*, 1938, p. 14 and Plate 1.

[21] De Terra, 1940, p. 46 and Plate 13.

[22] S. Hummel, "Die heilige Höhle in Tibet", *Anthropos*, 52, 1957, pp. 623 ff.

[23] Waddell, 1905, p. 289.

[24] Tucci and Ghersi, 1934, pp. 329 ff., and Tucci, *Santi...*, 1937, pp. 168–75.

[25] R. de Nebesky-Wojkowitz, "Ancient funeral ceremonies of the Lepchas", *Eastern Anthropologist*, 5, 1951, pp. 23 ff.

[26] Tucci, *To Lhasa*, 1956, p. 106.

[27] Tucci, *Santi...*, 1937, pp. 118 ff.

[28] Stacul, 1969.

[29] Pelliot, 1961, p. 2.

[30] Francke, 1914, vol. I, p. 22, fig. (b), *right*, and Tucci, 1966, p. 59.

[31] Tucci, *Santi...*, 1937, p. 49.
[32] *Ibid.*, p. 65.
[33] *Ibid.*, p. 16. fig. (a).
[34] Roerich, 1933, Plate XLIII.
[35] *Ibid.*, p. 235.
[36] *Ibid.*
[37] S. Hummel, "Die Steinringe des tibetischen Megalithicums und die Gesar-saga", *Anthropos*, 60, 1965, p. 833.
[38] A.W. Macdonald, "Une note sur les mégalithes tibétains", *Journal Asiatique*, 1953, pp. 63 ff.
[39] Bacot, 1909, p. 191.
[40] Roerich, 1933, p. 246.
[41] *Ibid.*, p. 236.
[42] *Ibid.*, p. 105.
[43] R. Stein, "Les K'iang des marches sino-tibétaines", *Annuaire de l'Ecole Pratique des Hautes Etudes*, 1957–58, Section des Religions, Paris, 1957, p. 4.
[44] Aufschnaiter, 1956, p. 74.
[45] *Ibid.*, p. 75.
[46] *Ibid.*, p. 81.
[47] Francke, 1914, pp. 72 ff.
[48] Francke refers to M.H. Duncan, *A Summer Ride through Western Tibet*, p. 148, which I have been unable to obtain.
[49] "The animal style among the nomad tribes of Northern Tibet", *Skythika, Seminarium Kondakovianum*, Prague, 1930, p. 30.
[50] *Ibid.*, third fig. after p. 96.
[51] Tucci, *Santi...*, 1937, p. 106, figs. 1–14.
[52] *Bulletin of Tibetology*, vol. 4, No. 1, p. 8.
[53] Bacot, etc., 1940, p. 60.
[54] The word *ke ke ru* is referred to in Laufer, 1916, where it is defined as meaning "cat's eye, chrysoberyl", and is also discussed in Laufer, 1913, p. 162. The derivation suggested is from Prakrit *kakkeraa* or Sanskrit *karketana*.
[55] The one at Shapgeding, situated on the summit of a mountain, is the most imposing example I have seen.
[56] Tucci, 1966, p. 50.
[57] Bacot, etc., 1940, pp. 109–47.
[58] Tucci, *Santi...*, 1937, p. 136.
[59] S. Hummel, "Der Ursprung des tibetischen Mandalas", *Ethnos*, 1958, pp. 158 ff.
[60] Landon, 1898, p. 283; E. Olson, "More about Tibetan ceramics", *Far Eastern Ceramic Bulletin*, vol. 4, No. 3; W. Asboe, "Pottery in Ladakh", *Man*, 1946; S. Hummel, "Profane und religiöse Gegenstände aus Tibet und der lamaistischen Umwelt im Linden-Museum", *Tribus*, 1964, p. 32.

[61] J.F. Rock, "Excerpts from a history of Sikkim", *Anthropos*, 48, 1953, p. 945.
[62] R. de Nebesky-Wojkowitz, "Die Legende vom Turmbau der Lepchas", *Anthropos*, 48, 1953, pp. 879 ff.
[63] According to the same author, remains of a stone tower were discovered when the Daramdin plateau was being brought into cultivation.
[64] Tucci, 1932–41, vol. III, Plates 55 and 57. Cf. Francke, 1914, Plate XLIV, (a) and (b).
[65] Tucci, 1950.
[66] Pelliot, 1961, p. 3.
[67] Tucci, 1950, pp. 3 and 9.
[68] Ferrari, 1958, p. 52.
[69] Tucci, 1950, p. 10.
[70] Pelliot, 1961, p. 3, and Lalou, 1952.
[71] Tucci, 1950.
[72] Tucci, 1970, pp. 249–51.
[73] Richardson, 1953; Li Fan-Kuei, 1956.
[74] Richardson, 1952 and 1953.
[75] H.E. Richardson, *Journal of the Royal Asiatic Society*, 1954, p. 157.
[76] Pelliot, 1961, p. 2.
[77] *Ibid.*
[78] Ferrari, 1958, p. 101, No. 86.
[79] Tucci, 1950, pp. 83, 84; Tucci, *To Lhasa*, 1956, p. 140.
[80] Tucci, 1950, p. 22.
[81] See photograph in Stein, 1972.
[82] Ferrari, 1958, pp. 57, 108.
[83] Snellgrove and Richardson, 1968, photograph on p. 40; V.T. Wylie, "Mar-pa's tower. Notes on local hegemons in Tibet", *History of Religions*, 3, 1964, p. 278.
[84] On temples, see Richardson, 1952, fig. (a), p. 1, which shows certain affinities with Gandharan architecture.
[85] Tucci, 1950, p. 54.
[86] Roerich, 1949 and 1953, p. 184.
[87] Tucci, *To Lhasa*, 1956, p. 126; Tucci, 1950, p. 83.
[88] Tucci, *To Lhasa*, 1956, p. 106.
[89] Liu I-Ssu, 1957, Plates LXIII and LXIV.
[90] Tucci, *Preliminary Report*, 1956, pp. 66 ff.
[91] Cf. the beams supporting the roof of a Nepalese temple in G. Tucci, *Rati-Lila*, Geneva, 1969, plates on pp. 98 ff.
[92] Tucci, 1932–41, vol. 4, p. 3, Plate 36.
[93] Liu I-Ssu, 1957, Plate LV: Stein, 1972, Plates 28 and 29.

94 Tucci and Ghersi, 1934, p. 126.
95 Barrett, 1957, Plates 3–7. Cf. the two consorts of Viṣṇu in the temple of Avantisvāmin at Avantipur, who survived into later Kashmiri art.
96 Tucci, 1950, p. 51.
97 Vibhūticandra came to Tibet in the 13th century; Roerich, 1949 and 1953, pp. 600–01.
98 Tucci, 1950, Plate 3.
99 Tucci, *To Lhasa*, 1956, p. 120.
100 H.E. Richardson, "A Tibetan inscription from Rgyal Lha khaṅ and a note on Tibetan chronology from A.D. 841 to A.D. 1042", *Journal of the Royal Asiatic Society*, 1957, pp. 57 ff.
101 Tucci, *To Lhasa*, 1956, p. 145.
102 Tucci, *Santi...*, 1937, pp. 157 ff.
103 Tucci, "Indian painting", 1937, p. 191.
104 Reproduced in colour on back of jacket of Tucci, 1967.
105 On Citra, see Sivaramurti, *South Indian Paintings*, New Delhi, 1967.
106 Yazdani, 1930–55.
107 Tucci, 1932–41, vol. 2, p. 41.
108 *Ibid.*, p. 66.
109 *Ibid.*, p. 69.
110 *Ibid.*, vol. 3, p. 195, Plate XLVI.
111 *Ibid.*, vol. 4, Part I, p. 93.
112 *Ibid.*, p. 103.
113 For the inscription see Tucci, 1932–41, vol. 4, Part I, pp. 189 ff., and vol. 4, Part III, Plates 23 and 24.
114 *Archaeological Survey of India, Annual Report*, 1909–10, Calcutta, 1914, p. 18. The figure illustrated in Tucci, 1932–41, vol. 4, Part III, Plate 13, and another figure from Lhasa belong to the same school.
115 Tucci, 1932–41, vol. 4, Part III, Plates 15 ff.
116 Goetz, 1969, Plate XXV: temple of Markulā Devī in Lahul.
117 Tucci, *To Lhasa*, 1956, p. 145.
118 See below, p. 115.
119 Tucci, 1961.
120 Tucci, 1932–41, vol. 1.
121 See p. 115.
122 Tucci, 1970, pp. 72 ff.
123 Tucci, 1961.
124 Bhattasali, 1929, Plate X (b).
125 As can be seen from Tucci, 1932–41, vol. 1, Plate XXXI.
126 See p. 180.

[127] See p. 89.
[128] Ferrari, 1958, p. 64 and Note 50.
[129] *Ibid.*, 75–78.
[130] Tucci, 1949, p. 682.
[131] *Ibid.*, p. 173.
[132] Tucci, 1932–41, vol. 7, p. 70.
[133] Tucci, *To Lhasa*, 1956, p. 178.
[134] See p. 79.
[135] Obermiller, 1931, p. 184.
[136] Tucci, 1949, p. 278.
[137] Sumpakhenpo, 1908, p. 136.
[138] *sBa bzhed*, p. 71.
[139] *Chronicle of the Fifth Dalai Lama*, p. 26, (b).
[140] See above, p. 94.
[141] Tucci, 1959.
[142] See above, p. 94.
[143] Tucci and Ghersi, 1934, p. 302. For the decoration which runs round the lower part, see Toyo Bijutsu Ten, 1968, p. 146, Plate 34.
[144] E.g. Songtsengampo: Tucci, 1932–41, vol. 2, p. 66.
[145] Cf. recently Goetz, 1969, p. 73.
[146] Cf. Note 104.
[147] Tucci, *Santi...*, 1937, Plates 48 ff.
[148] *Ibid.*, p. 48.
[149] See above, p. 94.
[150] *Archaeological Survey of India, Annual Report*, 1914, Plate VIII.
[151] Tucci, 1932–41, vol.4, Part III, Plates XI, XII, XIX, XX, XXII, XLII, XLIII, XLIV and XLV.
[152] See p. 94.
[153] On the dress, see for example Erdmann, 1943, Plates LIXVII, LIXVIII and CI.
[154] Snellgrove and Richardson, 1968, plate on p. 256, below.
[155] Tucci, 1949, p. 172, Plate 2.
[156] *Ibid.*, p. 189.
[157] P. 87.
[158] Pal, 9169, No. 41.
[159] Tucci, 1932–41, vol. 5, Part I, pp. 142 ff., and vol. 4, Part III, Plates 62 and 63.
[160] Banerji, 1933, Plate LXXIV (b),.
[161] See above, p. 177.

162 Bhattasali, 1929, Plate XXIV; *Archaeological Survey of India, Annual Report*, 1930–1934, 1936, Part II, Plate CXXIV.
163 Tucci, 1932–41, vol.4, Part III, Plates 64 and 65; Bhattasali, 1929, Plate XVI; Banerji, 1933, Plate LXXII.
164 Cf. Tucci, 1949, vol. II.
165 For example in Tucci, 1949, Plate C, above. The four other figures in the same plate can be compared with those from Mangnang, particularly the second and the last in Plate D, which have the same relief and chiaroscuro effects as the paintings in this temple.
166 Tucci, 1932–41, vol. 4, Part III, p. 48.
167 Madanjeet Singh, 1968, pp. 47 and 60.
168 *Ibid.*, p. 39.
169 *Ibid.*, p. 63.
170 Tucci, 1932–41, vol. 4, Part III, Plates 46 *bis*, 48 and 51.
171 Tucci, 1949, Plate 28.
172 This *thangka* is reproduced in Tucci, 1949, and here by the courtesy of the Istituto Poligrafico dello Stato, Rome.
173 Tucci, 1949, Plate 78.
174 Tucci, 1932–41, vol. 4, Part III, Plate 51.
175 Banerjee, 1968, p. 114.
176 Le Coq and Waldschmidt, 1922–33, chapter 3, Plate VI.
177 *Ibid.*, Plate XX.
178 Bussagli, 1970, fig. (a), p. 45.
179 Tucci, 1949, vol. 1, p. 180, Plate 24.
180 Tucci, 1949, p. 157.
181 Plate 47 is reproduced by kind permission of Mr H.E. Richardson.
182 For example the base of the *doring* at Karchung *(sKar c'uṅ)*.
183 Waddell, 1905, p. 376.
184 Tucci, 1958.

COMPARATIVE CHRONOLOGY

DATE	IRAN	CHINA	CENTRAL ASIA	NEPAL	INDIA	TIBET
200	Sassanids (226–651)				Gupta dynasty (320–500)	
600	Arab conquest (637–651)	Sui dynasty (589–618) T'ang dynasty (618–906)	Hephthalite kingdom (4th–6th c.) Arab conquest of Merv (651)	Licchavi dynasty, under strong Gupta influence (2nd–7th c.) Thākuri dynasty founded by Aṃśuvarman	Toramāṇa (c. 490–512) Mihirakula (c. 512–528) Harṣa of Kanauj (606–647)	Songtsengampo (620–649) Songtsengampo's tomb (650) Progress in conquest of Central Asia (676–704)
700					Lalitaditya (713–750) Turki Shāhi dynasty (8th c.) Pāla dynasty (740–1125) Sena dynasty (11th c.) Gurjara Pratihāras (750–1036) Rashtrakūṭas (757–973)	Thisongdetsen (755–797?) Foundation of Samye monastery (715) Buddhism recognised as state religion (779)
800				New dynasty (879)	Hindu Shāhis (c. 885 to end of 10th c.)	Thitsukdetsen (Repacen) (815–838) Persecution of Buddhism (838–842) Violation of tombs of Tibetan kings (866)
900		Five dynasties (907–960)			Mahmud of Ghazni (998–1030)	Second expansion of Buddhism in Tibet (9th–10th c.) Rinchensangpo (958–1055) is sent into Kashmir

Year					
1000			Second Thākuri dynasty (11th c.)		Atiśa is invited into Tibet and dies at Nyethang, near Lhasa (1042) Foundation of Sakya monastery (1073)
1100	Seljuk dynasty (11th–13th c.)	Jenghis Khan (1167–1227)		Gāhaḍavāla dynasty (12th c.)	Marpa (d. 1098); foundation of Sekhar tower Foundation of Digung monastery (1179) Foundation of Tshurphu monastery (1189)
1200	Ilkhanid dynasty (beginning of 13th c. to mid 14th c.)		Malla dynasty (c. 1200)	Northern India under the Muslims	Jenghis Khan meets Tibetan dignitaries (1206) The Sakyapa become *Ti shih* of the Mongol kings
1300					Changchup-gyentsen (d. 1373) supplants the Sakyapa and established the authority of the Phagmotupa
1400	Ming dynasty (1368–1644)	Conquest of Balkh and Samarkand by Tamerlane (1370)	Jayasthiti Malla (c. 1380–1400) gives fresh impetus to the Malla dynasty		Foundation of Ganden (1409) Foundation of Depung (1416) Foundation of Sera (1419) Foundation of Tashilhünpo (1447)

BIBLIOGRAPHY

AN SHOU-JÊN, "Pa-ssu-pa chien hu pi lieh pi-hua", *Wên-wu*, Peking, 7, 1959, pp. 12-13.

Archaeological Survey of India, Annual Report, 59, 1907–08.

AUFSCHNAITER, P., "Prehistoric sites discovered in inhabited regions of Tibet", *East and West*, 7, 1956, p. 74.

sBa bzhed, ed. R.A. Stein, Paris, 1961.

BACOT, J., *Dans les marches tibétaines*, Paris, 1909.

BACOT, J., THOMAS, F.W. and TOUSSAINT, C., *Documents de Touen-houang relatifs à l'histoire du Tibet*, Paris, 1940.

BANERJEE, P., "Painted covers of two Gilgit manuscripts", *Oriental Art*, N.S. 14, 1968.

BANERJI, R.D., "Eastern Indian school of mediaeval sculpture", *Archaeological Survey of India*, New Imperial Series, Delhi, vol. 47, 1933.

BARRETT, D.,"Sculptures of the Shaki period", *Oriental Art*, N.S. 3, 1957, p. 54.

BARRETT, D., "The Buddhist art of Tibet and Nepal", *Oriental Art*, N.S. 3, 1957.

BELENITSKY, A., *Central Asia*, Geneva, 1968.

BHATTASALI, N.K., *Iconography of Buddhist and Brahmanical Sculptures in the Dacca Museum*, Dacca, 1929.

BUNKER, E., CHATWIN, C.B. and FARKAS, A.R., "Animal style", *Art from East to West*, Asia Society, 1970.

BUSSAGLI, M., "Bronze objects collected by Prof. G. Tucci in Tibet. A short survey of religious and magic symbolism", *Artibus Asiae*, 12, 1949, pp. 331-47.

BUSSAGLI, M., *Peinture de l'Asie Centrale*, Geneva, 1963.

BUSSAGLI, M., *Culture e civiltà dell'Asia Centrale*, Turin, 1970.

CHIANG CHENG-LIANG, "Pa T'ang Fan hui-meng pei", *Wên-wu*, Peking, pp. 9-11.

CHIANG LIN, "Kuan yü Chu Tsang ta-chen-ti-chi-chien wên-wu", *Wên-wu*, Peking, pp. 23-27.

Chronicle of the Fifth Dalai Lama (in Tibetan), xylograph, Lhasa, written in 1643.

CHU CHIA-CHIN, "Ku-kung so Tsang Ming Ch'ing liang-tai yu kuan Hsi-tsang ti wên-wu", *Wên-wu*, Peking, pp. 14-19.

CHU CHIA-YÜAN, "Hsi-huang-ssu hsieh Hsu-mi-lu shou-miao", *Wên-wu*, Peking, pp. 20-22.

DAUVILLIER, J., "Les provinces chaldéennes de 'l'Extérieur' au Moyen Age", *Mélanges Cavallera*, Toulouse, 1948, pp. 261-316.

DAUVILLIER, J., "L'expansion au Tibet de l'Eglise chaldéenne au Moyen Age et le problème des rapports du bouddhisme et du christianisme", *Bulletin de la Société toulousaine d'études classiques*, 79, Jan.-Feb. 1950, pp. 1-4.

DE TERRA, H., *Durch Urwelten am Indus*, Leipzig, 1940.

ERDMANN, K., *Die Kunst Irans zur Zeit der Sasaniden*, Berlin, 1943.

FERRARI, A., *mK'yen Brtse's Guide to the Holy Places of Central Tibet*, Rome, 1958.

FRANCKE, A.H., *The Antiquities of Indian Tibet*, 2 vols., Calcutta, 1914 and 1926.

GOETZ, H., "A late Pratihāra 'brass' group", *Oriental Art*, 2, 1956, p. 148.

GOETZ, H., "Studies in the history and art of Kashmir and the Indian Himalaya", *Schriftenreihe des Südasieninstituts*, Wiesbaden, 1969.

GOLDMAN, B., "Some aspects of the animal deity: Luristan, Tibet and Italy", *Ars Orientalis*, 4, 1961, pp. 287 ff.

GRISWOLD, A.B., KIM, C. and POTT, P.H., *The Art of Burma, Corea and Tibet*, London, 1964.

HAMBIS, L., "Notes sur quelques sceaux amulettes nestoriens en bronze", *Bulletin de l'Ecole française d'Extrême-Orient*, 44, 1954, pp. 483–525.

HEINE-GELDERN, R., "Das Tocharer-Problem und die pontische Wanderung", *Saeculum*, 1951, p. 225.

HU CHIA, "Yu Kuan Wên-ch'eng-kung chu-ti chi-chien wên-wu", *Wên-wu*, Peking, pp. 5–8.

K'ao-ku, Peking, 1959 onwards; new series, 1972 onwards.

K'ao-ku hsüeh-pao, Peking, 1959 onwards.

K'ao-ku t'ung-hsün, Peking, 1955 onwards.

KISELEV, S.V., *Drevnyaya istoriya yuzhnoy Sibiri* ("Ancient History of Southern Siberia"), Moscow and Leningrad, 1949.

KHANDAVALA, K., "Some Nepalese and Tibetan bronzes in the collection of Mr B.S. Sethna", *Mārg*, vol. 4, No.1.

LALOU, M., "Rituel Bon-po dans des funérailles royales", *Journal asiatique*, 38/3, 1952, pp. 275 ff.

LANDON, H.S., *In the Forbidden Land*, London, 1898, p. 283.

LAUFER, B., "Loan words in Tibetan", *T'oung Pao*, 17, 1916, p. 403.

LAUFER, B., *Dokumente der indischen Kunst: Das Citralakṣaṇa*, Leipzig, 1913.

LE COQ, A. von and WALDSCHMIDT, E., *Die buddhistische Spätantike in Mittelasien*, 7 parts, Berlin, 1922-23.

LI FAN-KUEI, "The inscription of the Sino-Tibetan treaty of 821-822", *T'oung Pao*, 44, 1956, p. 1.

LITVINSKY, B.A., *Arkheologicheskie otkrytiya na vostochnom Pamire i problema svyazey mezhdu Sredney Aziey, Kitaem i Indiey v drevnosti* ("Archaeological Discoveries in the Eastern Pamir and the Problem of the Connections between Central Asia, China and India in Ancient Times"), 25th International Congress of Orientalists, Moscow, 1960.

LIU I-SSU, "Hsi ts'ang Fo-chiao i-shu", *Wên-wu*, Peking, 1957.

MADANJEET SINGH, *Himalayan Art*, London, 1968. (Fine reproductions of objects from Lahul, Ladakh and Spiti; attribution and dating sometimes questionable).

MISSION PELLIOT III: *Douldour Agour et Soubachi*, Plates, ed. L. Hambis, Paris, 1967.

PELLIOT, P., *Histoire ancienne du Tibet*, Paris, 1961.

RICHARDSON, H.E., "Three ancient inscriptions from Tibet", *Journal of the Royal Asiatic Society*, 1949, pp. 45-65.

RICHARDSON, H.E., "Tibetan inscriptions at the *Zhva'i lha-khang*", *ibid.*, 1952, pp. 133-54, and 1953, pp. 1-12.

RICHARDSON, H.E., *Ancient Historical Edicts at Lhasa*, London, 1953.

RICHARDSON, H.E., "A ninth-century inscription from *rKong-po, ibid.*, 1954, pp. 57-73.

ROERICH, G. de, *Tibetan Paintings*, Paris, 1925.

ROERICH, G. de, *Sur les pistes de l'Asie Centrale*, Paris, 1933.

ROERICH, G. de, *The Blue Annals of gZhon-nu-dpal*, 2 vols., Calcutta, 1949 and 1953.

RUDENKO, S.I., "Die Kultur der Hsiung-nu und die Hügelgräber von Noin Ula", *Antiquitas*, Bonn, 7, 1969. (Translated from the Russian by Helmut Pollens; preface by Karl Jettmar).

SIREN, O., *A History of Early Chinese Art*, vol. 3, London, 1930.

SNELLGROVE, D. and RICHARDSON, H.E., *A Cultural History of Tibet*, London, 1968.

STACUL, G., "Excavations in a rock shelter near Ghālīgai (Swat, West Pakistan): Preliminary report", *East and West*, 17, 1967, pp. 185 ff.

STACUL, G., "Excavations near Ghālīgai (1968) and the chronological sequence of protohistorical cultures in the Swat valley (West Pakistan)", *ibid.*, 19, 1969, pp. 44 ff.

STEIN, R.A., *Tibetan Civilization*, London, 1972.

SUMPAKHENPO, *History of the Rise, Progress and Downfall of Buddhism in India*, ed. Sarat Chandra Das, Calcutta, 1908.

TADDEI, M., "Inscribed clay tablets and miniature stūpas from Ghazni", *East and West*, 20, 1970, pp. 70 ff. (Contains a rich bibliography).

TALLGREN, A.M., "Inner Asiatic and Siberian rock pictures", *Eurasia Septentrionalis Antiqua*, vol. 8, p. 187, figs. 17–22.

TŌYŌ BIJUTSU TEN, *Exhibition of Eastern Art celebrating the Opening of the Gallery of Eastern Antiquities*, National Museum, Tokyo, 1968.

TUCCI, G., *Indo-Tibetica*, 7 vols., Rome, 1932–41.

TUCCI, G., "On some bronze objects discovered in Western Tibet", *Artibus Asiae*, 5, 1935, pp. 105–116.

TUCCI, G., "Indian painting in Western Tibetan temples", *ibid.*, 8, 1937, p. 130.

TUCCI, G., *Santi e briganti nel Tibet ignoto*, Milan, 1937.

TUCCI, G., "Preistoria Tibetana", *Rivista di Antropologia*, 36, 1948, p. 265.

TUCCI, G., *Tibetan Painted Scrolls*, 3 vols., Rome, 1949.

TUCCI, G., *The Tombs of the Tibetan Kings*, Rome, 1950.

TUCCI, G., *Preliminary Report on two Scientific Expeditions in Nepal*, Rome, 1956.

TUCCI, G., *To Lhasa and Beyond*, Rome, 1956.

TUCCI, G., "Preliminary reports and studies on the Italian excavations in Swat (Pakistan)", *East and West*, 1958, p. 279.

TUCCI, G., "A Tibetan classification of the Buddhist images according to their style", *Artibus Asiae*, 22, 1959, pp. 179 ff.

TUCCI, G., *Discovery of the Mallas*, London, 1962.

TUCCI, G., *Tibetan Folk Songs from Gyantse and Western Tibet*, Ascona, 1966.

TUCCI, G., *Tibet: Land of Snows*, London, 1967.

TUCCI, G., *Theory and Practice of the Mandala*, London, 1969.

TUCCI, G., "Die Religionen Tibets", in TUCCI and HEISSIG, *Die Religionen Tibets und der Mongolei*, Stuttgart, 1970.

TUCCI, G. and GHERSI, G., *Cronaca della missione scientifica Tucci nel Tibet Occidentale*, Rome, 1934.

VOGEL, J.P., "Antiquities of Chamba State", *Archaeological Survey of India*, N.S. 36, Part I, Calcutta, 1911.

WADDELL, L.A., *Lhasa and its Mysteries*, London, 1905.

Wên-wu, Peking, 1959 onwards. Ceased publication 1966; new series started 1971.

YAZDANI, G., *Ajanta: Colour and Monochrome Reproductions of the Ajanta Frescoes based on Photographs*, with an introduction by L. Binyon, 4 vols., London, 1930–55.

LIST OF ILLUSTRATIONS

1 Brass plaque with symbols of the twelve animals of the sixty-year cycle (based on the alternation of the five elements – water, earth, fire, wood and metal – and twelve animals – the ox, the mouse, the bird, etc.), with Buddhist symbols above. Period after the introduction of Buddhism. From Miang *(Ma yaṅ?)*, western Tibet. Bonardi collection.

2 Bronze belt buckles. Pre-Buddhist period. From Tsaparang, western Tibet. Bonardi collection.

3 Bronze amulet with figures of stylised animals. Pre-Buddhist period. From Tholing. Bonardi collection.

4 Bronze objects of sacred significance. Pre-Buddhist period. From Lake Manasarovar. Bonardi collection.

5 Bronze objects of sacred significance. Date of upper items uncertain; others pre-Buddhist. From Yarlung, central Tibet. Bonardi collection.

6 Bronze objects of sacred significance, consisting of two, three or thirteen circles; the object *below*, *left*, is of doubtful significance. Pre-Buddhist period. From Lake Manasarovar. Bonardi collection.

7 *Left*, belt buckle (?). Pre-Buddhist period. From Lake Manasarovar. *Right*, ring of sacred significance. Pre-Buddhist period. Bonardi collection.

8 Objects of sacred significance. 9th–8th centuries B.C. From Luristan, Iran. (Compare with Plate 3).

9 Bronze circle of ritual or magical significance. Pre-Buddhist period. From western Tibet. Bonardi collection.

10 Triangular bronze amulets. Pre-Buddhist period. From Yarlung. Bonardi collection.

11	Bronze figurines of the *khyung*; the one farthest left, below, may represent a dove and accordingly may be Nestorian. Yüan period (1276–1368). From Miang, western Tibet. Bonardi collection.
12	Bronze figurine, possibly of a bear; the ring at the end of the muzzle suggests that it may have been a talisman. Period uncertain. From Sakya. Bonardi collection.
13	Handle or terminal in the form of a stylised ram's head. Pre-Buddhist period. From Shigatse. Bonardi collection. (Cf. Bunker, Chatwin and Farkas, Plate 73).
14	Bronze figurine of an offering-bearer. Pre-Buddhist period. From Chonggye, central Tibet. Bonardi collection.
15	*Right*, hook or ear-pick (?); *left*, unidentifiable object. Pre-Buddhist period. From western Tibet. Bonardi collection.
16	Circular bronze pendant. Pre-Buddhist period. Bonardi collection. (Cf. Plates 3–8).
17	Bronze figurine of a monkey; worn suspended as a talisman. Period uncertain. From Tsaparang, western Tibet. Bonardi collection.
18	The same: front view.
19	Bronze amulet representing four linked birds, each having a single body and two heads. Pre-Buddhist period. From Shigatse. Bonardi collection.
20	The same: view from above.
21	The same: side view.
22	Bronze ball with suspension eyelet. Period uncertain. From western Tibet. Bonardi collection.

23   Bronze ball. Period uncertain. From western Tibet. Bonardi collection.

24   Unidentified bronze object. The head in the centre indicates that it cannot be a fibula but suggests that it may be of religious significance. Pre-Buddhist period. From Lake Manasarovar. Bonardi collection.

25   Object representing two animals standing erect *(left)* and a stylised animal's head *(right)*. Pre-Buddhist period. From Lake Manasarovar. Bonardi collection.

26   Pendant of uncertain significance, perhaps a small bell. Pre-Buddhist period. From Shigatse. Bonardi collection.

27   Bronze figurine of *Bos indicus*. Pre-Buddhist period. From Mount Kailāsa area. Bonardi collection.

28   Bronze figurine of a feline. Pre-Buddhist period. From Sakya area. Bonardi collection.

29   Bronze pendants in the shape of a cross. Probably Nestorian and therefore of the Yüan period (1276–1368). From Lhatse. Bonardi collection.

30   Bronze fibula. Pre-Buddhist period. From Gartok, western Tibet. Bonardi collection.

31   Bronze fibula. Date uncertain. From Lake Manasarovar. Bonardi collection.

32   Objects of uncertain significance; the one *below*, *left*, ends in three heads (human or animal). Pre-Buddhist period. From Lhatse. Bonardi collection.

33	Iron arrowheads. Period uncertain. From Sakya. Bonardi collection.
34	Caves near Lhatse, Tsang. Period uncertain; probably prehistoric.
35	Caves at Janthang *(Byaṅ t'aṅ?)*. Prehistoric period.
36	Caves near Lake Yanḍogtsho, central Tibet. Probably prehistoric period.
37	Caves at Yarlung, southern Tibet. Probably prehistoric period.
38	Megaliths near Dopṭadsong, Tsang. Probably pre-Buddhist period.
39	"Tomb of the Ascetic", near Lake Manasarovar. Pre-Buddhist period.
40	Bonpo tombs at Lo (*Blo*, between Tibet and Nepal). Period uncertain.
41	Tomb near Lake Yanḍogtsho, central Tibet. Probably prehistoric period.
42	Tomb near Shigatse, Tsang. Probably prehistoric period.
43	Edict by Ṭhidesongtsen (755–797) inscribed on pillar in front of temple at Samye, central Tibet, proclaiming Buddhism the state religion.
44	Tombs of the Tibetan kings at Chonggye, south of the Tsangpo; to rear, tomb of Songtsengampo (d. 649). After Ferrari, Plate 31. (Ph. H.E. Richardson).
45	Pillar of a royal tomb at Chonggye.

46   Pillar of Ṭhidesongtsen's tomb, Chonggye.

47   Stone lion near tomb of Repachen (815–838) at Chonggye. To rear, Songtsengampo's tomb.

48   Yumbulhakhar palace, south of the Tsangpo. 4th century.

49   The Sekhar tower in Lhoṭak, built by Milarepa (1040–1123) for his teacher Marpa (d. 1098). After Ferrari, Plate 39. (Ph. H.E. Richardson).

50   Loopholes in wall of castle at Luk, western Tibet. 10th–11th century.

51   Castle at Nü, western Tibet. 10th–11th century (?).

52   Castle at Penam *(sPa snam)*, Tsang. The tower probably dates from the 12th century.

53   Monastery of Ṭashigang *(bKra šis sgaṅ)*, western Tibet, built on the ruins of an earlier castle. 11th–12th century. In centre, round tower.

54   Ruins of old castles in western Tibet. 10th–11th centuries.

55   Apsidal building at Kampadsong *(sGam pa rdsoṅ)*. 11th–12th century (?).

56   Castle at Tsaparang, western Tibet, from above. 11th–15th centuries.

57   Ruins of castle at Pelkye *(dPal rgyas?)*, western Tibet. 10th–11th century.

58   Ruins of castle at Khyunglung *(K'yuṅ luṅ)*. The original structure dates from the 8th–9th century.

59 Iron bridge over the Kyichu *(sKyid c'u)* attributed to Thangton gyelpo *(T'aṅ ston rGyal po)* (1385–1464). (Ph. H.E. Richardson).

60 Ruins of monastery at Nesar, Tsang. 8th century.

61 Temple at Mangnang, western Tibet. 11th century.

62 Small chapel, western Tibet. 12th century.

63 General view of Samye, central Tibet. 8th century.

64 Entrance of temple at Samada, Tsang. 12th century.

65 General view of Tholing, western Tibet. Monastery founded by Rinchensangpo (958–1053).

66 Exterior of chapel at Ushangdo *(U šaṅ rdo)*. 9th century.

67 Pillar inside chapel at Ushangdo. 9th century.

68 Initiation temple at Tholing. 11th century.

69 Statue in stucco. 11th–12th century. From Tiak *(gTi yag?)*, western Tibet.

70 Statue of Chenresik *(sPyan ras gzigs)* by Mati, a pupil of Rinchensangpo. 11th–12th century. From Samada, Tsang.

71 General view of Sakya monastery (founded 1073).

72 Detail of roof of temple at Zhalu *(Ža lu)*, founded in Yüan period (1276–1368).

73 The same.

74 Porch of temple at Samada. 11th–12th century.

75 Wall paintings from a temple, showing different types of *chöten*. 14th–15th century. From western Tibet.

76 *Chötens* near Ṭhanṭuk *(K'ra ạbrug)*. 13th century.
77 *Chötens* (restored) at Rapgyeling *(Rab rgyas gliṅ)*, western Tibet. 14th–15th century.
78 *Chöten* at Gyang *(rGyaṅ)*, Tsang. 14th–15th century.
79 The same: detail.
80 *Chöten* at Gyantse *(rGyal rtse)*, Tsang. 14th century.
81 *Chöten* at Champaling *(Byams pa gliṅ)*, central Tibet. 15th century.
82 Row of 108 *stūpas* at Milam *(rMi lam?)*, near Mangnang. 11th–12th century.
83 *Chöten* at Narthang, Tsang. 14th century.
84 *Chöten* at Tholing, traditionally believed to contain the remains of Rinchensangpo (958–1055).
85 *Chöten* near Samye. 8th–9th century.
86 Ruins of *chöten* near Khangsar *(K'aṅ gsar)*, western Tibet. 12th–13th century.
87 *Chöten* of gilded bronze. T'ang period (619–906). From the monastery of Ngariṭatsang *(mNa' ris grwa ts'aṅ)*, central Tibet.
88 Bronze *chöten*. 13th–14th century. From Ngariṭatsang monastery.
89 *Chöten* of sun-dried earth of the "descent from heaven" type. 12th–13th century. From Tholing, western Tibet.
90 The same. Bonardi collection.
91 *Chöten* of sun-dried earth of the "many doors" type. 12th–13th century. From Tsaparang, western Tibet. Bonardi collection.

225

92 The same. 11th–12th century. From Tholing, western Tibet.

93 Three *chötens* of sun-dried earth of the "descent from heaven" type, with formula from the Prajñāpāramitā. 12th–13th century. From western Tibet. Bonardi collection.

94 *Chöten* of the "descent from heaven" type, flanked by two smaller *stūpas*, with formula from the Prajñāpāramitā. 12th–13th century. From Dopṭakdsong *(rDo brag rdsoṅ)*, Tsang. Bonardi collection.

95 Large *chöten* flanked by two smaller ones: a souvenir from some famous monastery. 13th century.

96 Five *chötens* of sun-dried earth, above formulae from the Prajñāpāramitā. 11th–12th century. From western Tibet. Bonardi collection.

97 *Chöten* with door, surrounded by smaller *stūpas*. 13th–14th century. From Tholing, western Tibet. Bonardi collection.

98–99 *Ts'a ts'as* in the form of *chötens*. 12th century. From Sakya. Bonardi collection.

100 *Ts'a ts'a* of sun-dried earth representing Dorjesempa *(rDo rje sems dpa')*. 12th–13th century. From Sakya. Bonardi collection.

101 *Ts'a ts'a* of sun-dried earth representing the Bodhisattva Mañjuśrī. 13th century. From Lhatse, Tsang. Bonardi collection.

102 *Ts'a ts'a* of sun-dried earth representing Dorjesempa *(rDo rje sems dpa')*. 12th–13th century. From Tsang. Bonardi collection.

103 *Ts'a ts'a* of sun-dried earth representing the Bodhisattva Lokeśvara. 11th–12th century. From Zhalu, Tsang. Bonardi collection.

104 The same. From Tholing. Bonardi collection.

105   *Ts'a ts'a* of sun-dried earth representing Ḍölma (Tārā). 11th–12th century. From Tsaparang, western Tibet. Bonardi collection.

106   *Ts'a ts'a* of sun-dried earth representing the Bodhisattva Lokeśvara. 11th–12th century. From Chang, western Tibet. Bonardi collection.

107   *Ts'a ts'a* of sun-dried earth representing the Buddha Śākyamuni. 13th–14th century. From Tholing, western Tibet. Bonardi collection.

108   *Ts'a ts'a* of sun-dried earth representing Buddha between two Bodhisattvas. About 12th century. From western Tibet. Bonardi collection.

109   Gilded bronze plaque showing the Buddha cutting off his hair with a sword; beside him the gods Brahmā and Indra. 12th century. From Lhasa.

110   Bronze bell from Ṭhanṭuk *(K'ra ạbrug)*. 8th–9th century.

111   Iron vessel with inlaid ornament. Yüan period. From Sakya. Bonardi collection.

112   Large iron corn-measure with silver decoration: note the Nestorian cross. From Lhasa. Bonardi collection.

113   Wall painting from Mangnang: an *apsaras*. 11th–12th century.

114   The same: an ascetic.

115–117   The same: goddesses personifying offerings *(mc'od pai lha mo)*.

118   The same: Acala and Vajrapāṇi.

119   The same: Akṣobhya in the *bhūmisparśamudrā* posture.

120	The same: probably Vajradharma, a divinity of the Kunrik *(Kun rig)* cycle.
121	The same: a monk.
122	The same: detail from a wall painting.
123	Wall painting from Gyang: an offering-bearer. 14th century.
124	Figure of a Bodhisattva. 12th century. From chapel of Tshepame *(Ts'e dpag med)*, Iwang.
125	Wall paintings from Alchi, Ladakh: details from the life of the Buddha. 12th–13th century.
126	Carved beams in temple at Samada, Tsang. 12th century.
127	Large bronze statue of Vajrapāṇi. 11th–12th century. From Tholing. Kashmiri school.
128	Ivory statue of a Bodhisattva. Period of Rinchensangpo (958–1055). From Mangnang.
129	Buddha and two Bodhisattvas: wood. 11th century. From Tabo, Spiti.
130	Fragment of a terracotta Buddha. 11th century. From Tholing. Bonardi collection.
131	Wooden figure of a lion from the initiation temple at Tholing. Bonardi collection.
132	The same: detail.
133	Detail from carved wooden doorway. 11th–12th century. From Tsaparang, western Tibet.
134	Carved wood decoration from façade of monastery at Alchi, Ladakh. 11th–12th century.

135	The same: detail.
136	Fragment of a wooden doorway with scenes from the life of the Buddha. 11th century. From Tholing.
137	Wooden doorway with figures of the river goddesses of the Gaṅgā and the Yamunā. 12th cneutry. From temple of Gayādhara, Lhatse.
138	Wooden doorway. 11th–12th century. From Tsaparang.
139	Decoration of carved wood from façade of monastery at Alchi. 11th–12th century.
140	Fragment of gilded bronze nimbus with scenes from the life of the Buddha. 11th–12th century. From the Jampalhakhang *(aJams pai lha k'aṅ)*, Narthang.
141	Fragment of gilded nimbus with figure of Padmapāṇi and floral motifs. 11th–12th century. From Nanying.
142	Wood carving of a Bodhisattva. 11th–12th century. From Tabo.
143	Mārīcī: bronze statue. 10th–11th century. From Sakya. Pāla school. Bonardi collection.
144	Buddha Śākyamuni: wood statue. 11th–12th century. From Luk. Bonardi collection.
145	The Bodhisattva Padmapāṇi: bronze statue. 11th–12th century. Bonardi collection.
146	The Bodhisattva Padmapāṇi: bronze statue. 11th–12th century. From Tsaparang, but of Kashmiri origin. Bonardi collection.
147	The same. From Kojarnāth, western Tibet. Bonardi collection.

148–149	Illuminated manuscript of the *Prajñāpāramitā*. 11th century. Nepalese school. Bonardi collection.
150	Goddess *(apsaras)*: wood statue. 11th century. From Alchi. Bonardi collection.
151	The Bodhisattva Avalokiteśvara. 11th century. From Sakya. Pāla school. Bonardi collection.
152	The Bodhisattva Vajradharma. 10th–11th century. From Kongardsong *(Goṅ dkar rdsoṅ)*, Tsang. Pāla school. Bonardi collection.
153	Bronze statue of the goddess Kurukullā. 10th–11th century. From Sakya. Pāla school. Bonardi collection.
154	Bronze statue of Avalokiteśvara. 11th–12th century. From Chambā. Bonardi collection.
155	Buddha in the *bhūmisparśamudrā* posture. 12th–13th century. From Luk. Bonardi collection.
156	Nimbus of gilded wood. 14th–15th century. From Tsaparang. Kashmiri influence. Bonardi collection.
157	Bronze statues. Pāla period (10th–11th century). From Sakya monastery.
158	Bronze statues. The one in the centre is of the Pāla period (10th–11th century). From Sakya monastery.
159	Terracotta statue of Buddha. 10th–11th century. From Nesar, Tsang.
160	Bronze statue of Padmapāṇi. 12th century. From Pökhang *(sPos k'aṅ)* monastery, Tsang.

161 Bronze statue of a Bodhisattva. 12th–13th century. From Zinchi *(rDsiṅ p'yi)* monastery, central Tibet.

162 Plaster statue of a Bodhisattva. 11th–12th century. From Nesar monastery.

163 Plaster statue of a Bodhisattva. 11th–12th century. From Iwang monastery.

164 Chapel at Tholing containing statues of different periods; the one on the left, in bronze, is probably of Kashmiri origin. 11th–12th century.

165 Silver rim of a shell. Indian work. 10th–11th century. From Pökhang *(sPos k'aṅ)* monastery.

166 Bronze statue of Padmapāṇi with eyes inlaid in silver. 10th–11th century. From Ngor *(Ṅor)*. Bonardi collection.

167 Gilded bronze base of *chöten*. 12th–13th century. From Sakya monastery. (After *Tibetan Painted Scrolls*, by kind permission of the Istituto Poligrafico dello Stato, Rome).

168 The same. 11th–12th century.

169 Gilded bronze base of *chöten*. 11th century (?). From monastery at Narthang.

170 *Maṇḍala* in the form of a celestial palace. 12th–13th century. From Sakya.

171 Corner of a *chöten* in gilded copper. 12th century. From Samada.

172 Buddha: gilded bronze. 15th century. From Nyethang *(sNe t'aṅ)*.

173 Upper part of a gilded bronze nimbus. 12th–13th century. From Sakya monastery.

174	The same.
175	Statues of Tārā. Attributed to period of Atīśa (11th century). From temple at Nyethang.
176	Bronze statue of the Bodhisattva Padmapāṇi. 13th century. From Narthang.
177	The "royal robe" *(gyellukcho, rGyal lugs c'os)*, worn by the Tibetan kings and preserved in old families. (Ph. H.E. Richardson)
178	The Paolönchen *(dpa' bo Blon c'en)* at Nyethang, near Lhasa: believed to be the upper part of the body of Ḍanka-pelkiyonten *(Bran ka dPal gyi yon tan)*, a monk and minister of the time of Repachen. (Ph. H.E. Richardson).
179	The "ancient jewels" *(ringyen, riṅ rgyan)* worn by the Tibetan kings, according to a tradition which is still preserved. (Ph. H.E. Richardson).
180	Chinese fabric of the Yüan period (1276–1368). From Sakya monastery. Bonardi collection.
181	Cotton fabric with representations of the *stūpa* of Svayambhūnāth surrounded by winged figures of adorers. Nepalese work. From Narthang monastery. 16th century. Bonardi collection.
182	Wall paintings from *chöten* at Gyang: cycle of the Peldenlhamo *(dPal ldan lha mc)*. 15th-16th century.
183	Wall paintings from *chöten* at Gyang. 15th–16th century.
184	Wall paintings from *chöten* at Jonang *(Jo naṅ)*. 14th century.
185	Wall paintings from *chöten* at Gyang. 15th–16th century.
186–189	The same. 14th–15th century.

190–191   Wall paintings from *chöten* at Narthang.

192–196   Wall paintings from chapel of Shemar *(gŠed dmar)*, Phüntshokling *(P'un ts'ogs gliṅ)*. 16th century.

197   Sculpture of an Arhat. 14th century (?). From Norbukhyungtse *(Nor bu k'yuṅ rtse)*.

198   Stucco figure of Buddha. 12th–13th century. From Mangnang, western Tibet.

199   Rock bas-relief carving of Buddha. Period uncertain. Near Lhasa.

200   The same. 13th–14th century.

201   Stucco figure of Buddha. 13th–14th century. From Zhalu.

202   *Thangka:* Nangparnangse *(rNam par snaṅ mdsad)* (Vairocana) in the *vitarka-mudrā* posture. Nepalese school. From Narthang. Museum of Oriental Art, Rome. (After *Tibetan Painted Scrolls*, by kind permission of the Istituto Poligrafico dello Stato, Rome).

203   *Thangka:* Sakyapa lama. Nepalese school. From Ngor *(Ṅor)*. Museum of Oriental Art, Rome. (By kind permission of the Museum).

204   Fragment of *thangka:* Chamsing *(btsan lcam sriṅ)*, also known as Beg tse; on his left Rigpelhamo *(Rig pai lha mo)*, on his right Sogdak *(Srog bdag)*, surrounded by his eight acolytes (the *ḍithoks, gri t'ogs)*, brandishing swords. Nepalese school. From Lhatse. Museum of Oriental Art, Rome. (After *Tibetan Painted Scrolls*, by kind permission of the Istituto Poligrafico dello Stato, Rome).

205 *Thangka:* Ḍöljang *(sGrol ljaṅ)* (Syāmā Tārā), with right hand in the *varadamudrā* position and left hand in the *abhayamudrā*, between Recikma *(Ral gcig ma)* on the left and Mārīcī on the right. Above is a small image of Amitābha. The *thangka* also shows the different forms of Tārā and other representations of the group. Nepalese school. From Narthang. Museum of Oriental Art, Rome. (After *Tibetan Painted Scrolls*, by kind permission of the Istituto Poligrafico dello Stato, Rome).

206 *Thangka:* Dorjejiche *(rDo rje ajigs byed)* (Vajrabhairava), surrounded by the eight cemeteries, with figures of lamas. Nepalese school. From Narthang. Museum of Oriental Art, Rome. (After *Tibetan Painted Scrolls*, by kind permission of the Istituto Poligrafico dello Stato, Rome).

207 *Thangka:* Saṃvara. Nepalese school. From Sakya. Museum of Oriental Art, Rome.

208 *Thangka:* Buddha Śākyamuni in the *bhūmisparśamudrā* posture. Kashmiri school. From Luk monastery. Museum of Oriental Art, Rome.

209 *Thangka:* the 84 *siddhas*. The two central figures cannot be identified in the absence of inscriptions. Round them are the *siddhas*. The theme of this *thangka* is taken from the *bsTan agyur*, LXXII, 52: *Grub t'ob brgyad cu rstsa bžii gsol abeds*. Museum of Oriental Art, Rome. (After *Tibetan Painted Scrolls*, by kind permission of the Istituto Poligrafico dello Stato, Rome).

210 *Thangka:* Vajrapāṇi (?). Nepalese school. From monastery at Ngor. Museum of Oriental Art, Rome.

INDEX

(Figures in italics refer to illustrations)

abhayamudrā 205
Acala *118*
Afghanistan 56, 74, 117, 143
Ajaṇṭa 92
Akaramati 138
Akṣobhya *119*
Akṣobhyavajra 138
Alchi 53, 92, 143, 181, 182, *125, 134, 135, 139, 150*
Amitābha *205*
aṇḍa 113
apsaras 79, 92, *113, 150*
Arhats 15, 194, *197*
Asia, Central 15, 40, 62, 74, 116, 119, 137, 140, 142–4, 179, 181–3, 194, 199, 200
Asia, South-East 54, 180
aṣṭadhātu 177, 179
Atiśa 178, 180, *170*
Aufschnaiter, P. 52, 58
Avalokiteśvara 93, 138, 196, *151, 154*

Bacot, J. 52
Bajaurā 94, 144
Balalyk Tepe 181
Balukhar *(Ba lu mk'ar?)* 53
Bangsomarpo *(Baṅ so dmar po)* 61
Ba ri 138
Bäzälik 182–3
Beck, H.C. 40
Beg tse *204*
Bengal(i) 15, 94, 118, 139, 177–9, 200
Bharhut 113
Bhitaka *(Bi ta ka?)* 143
bhūmisparśamudrā 119, 155, 208
Bitpala *(Vidyāpāla?)* 139
bKa' ḁgyur (Buddha) 116
Bodhgayā 138
Bodhisattva 78, 94, 115, 118, 142, 144, 180, 199, *100–*
103, 106, 108, 124, 128, 129, 142, 145, 146, 151, 152, 161–163, 176
Bodhnāth 113
Bon: *see* Bonpo
Bonardi collection *1–7, 9–33, 90, 91, 93, 94, 96–108, 111, 112, 130–132, 143–156, 166, 180, 181*
Bonpo 34, 36, 57, 73, 183, *40*
Bos indicus 38, *27*
Brahmā *109*
Brahmaputra (Tsangpo) 54
Brahmin *(bram ze rigs)* 93
Brittany 51
bsTan ḁgyur 209
Buddha (Śākyamuni) 89, 93, 94, 113, 115, 116, 118, 142–3, 178, 180, 181, 193, 195, 196, 199, *107–109, 125, 129, 130, 136, 140, 155, 159, 172, 198–201, 208*
Buddhagupta 194
Buddhism, Buddhist 33, 38, 39, 55, 57, 59, 61, 64, 73, 77–80, 89, 90, 113, 115, 117–20, 137, 142–3, 177, 179, 180, 194, 199, *1, 43*
bum pa 113
Burma 117–8
Bussagli, M. 34
Byi'u 51

Carnac 51
chag-ri (lcags ri) 64
Chambā 79, 144, *154*
Champaling *(Byams pa gliṅ)* 119, *81*
Chamsing *(btsan lcam srin) 204*
Chang *(P'yaṅ* or *P'yi dbaṅ gdan mk'ar?)* 40, 49, 73, 92, 143, *106*
changchup-chöten *(byaṅ c'ub mc'od rten)* 113
Channadorje *(P'yag na rdo rje)* 93

chapo (bya po) 37
Chasa *(Bya sa)* 144
Chenresik *(sPyan ras gzigs)* 39, 93, *70*
Ch'iang 52
China, Chinese 14, 15, 33, 35, 39, 50, 55, 58, 61, 64, 74–9, 90, 95, 116, 137–8, 141–2, 177, 184, 193–5, 197, 200
Chin Ch'eng 78
Chingpataktse *(P'yin pa sTag rtse)* 74
Chögyel *(C'os rgyal)* 89, 119, 141
chökyong (c'os skyoṅ) 115
Chölotö *(C'os blo gros)* 93
Chonggye *(ḁ P'yoṅ rgyas)* 61, 74, *14î 44–47*
chöten (mc'od rten) 59, 74, 77, 94, 96, 113–20, 142, 179, 180, 182, 193–4, *75–98, 167–169, 171, 182–191*
Chotsho 183
Chushul *(C'u šul)* 196
citta 114

Ḍakinī 51
Dalai Lama 15, 79, 140
Ḍalha *(dGra lha)* 57
Ḍanang *(Dra naṅ* or *Drva naṅ)* 91, 94, 144
Ḍanka-pelkiyonten *(Bran ka dPal gyi yon tan) 178*
Danrayuntsho *(Dan rva yu mts'o)* 52
Daramdin plateau 58
Dards 54
Demosa *(bDe mo sa)* 64
Depung *(ḁBras spuṅs)* 90
Devapāla 139
Dhānyakataka 90
dhāraṇi 115
Dharmamati 93
Dharmapāla 139
dharmaśarīra 115
Dhīmān 139

235

Digumtsenpo *(Gri gum btsan po)* 63
Dinnāga 115
ḍithok (gri t'ogs) 204
Ḍöljang *(sGrol ljaṅ)* 205
Ḍölma pass 55
Ḍölma (Tārā, *sGrol ma*) 138, *105*
Ḍölmahakhang *(sGrol ma lha k'aṅ)* 138
dom 37
Dopṭakdsong *(rDo brag rdsoṅ)* 40, 51, *94*
doring (rdo riṅ) 51, 56–7, 80, 90, 196
Dorjejiche *(rDo rje ạjigs byed)* 206
Dorjesempa *(rDo rje sems dpa')* *100, 102*
dred 37

Euro-Asiatic 58

Francke, A.H. 53–4, 83

Gadong *(dGa' sdoṅ)* 138
Gandharan 77, 80, 114
Gaṅgā (Ganges) 143, *137*
Ganges 117, 179, 200
Garbyang 51, 56
Gartok *30*
Garuḍa 36
gau 39
Gayādhara 49, 143, *137*
Ghaznavid 180
Ghazni 180
Ghikö *(Gi k'od, Ge k'od)* 38
Gilgit 116, 119, 183, 196
Godan 90
Goldman, B. 34
Gonpo *(mGon po)* 137
gtso bo 91
Gujars 50
Gyamda *(rGya mda')* 55
Gyang *(rGyaṅ)* 119, 181–3, 78, 79, *123, 182, 183, 185*

Gyantse *(rGyal rtse)* 119, 144, *80*
Gyellhakhang *(rGyal lha k'aṅ)* 90
gyellokchö *(rGyal lugs c'os)* 177

Hambis, L. 38
Hanupat 54
Harrer, H. 52
Harvan 92
Hasarāja 139
Has po ri 74
Heine-Geldern, R. 35
Hellenistic 177
Hevajra 93
Himalayan 144, 200
Hindu Shāhī 140, 177, 180
Horpa 54
Hsiao-hsin 195
Hsi-ts'ang fu chiao i shu 178
Hummel, S. 35

India(n) 15, 38, 40, 58, 80, 90, 93–4, 113, 116–9, 137–40, 143–4, 177–80, 183, 194, 196, 199, 200, *165*
Indo-Tibetica 13
Indra *109*
Indus 53–4
Iran(ian) 34, 36–7, 40, 53, 180–1, 200, *8*
Islam(ic) 50, 143, 180
Istituto Poligrafico dello Stato, Rome *167, 202, 204–206, 209*
Iwang 79, 91, 93–4, 140, 144, 182, *124, 163*

Jain 177
Jambudvīpa 89
Jampalhakhang *(ạJams pai lha k'aṅ)* 140
Jampel *(ạJam dpal)* 76
Jamyang *(ạJam dbyaṅs)* 93
Janthang *(Byaṅ t'aṅ?)* 40, 35

Jäschke 55
Jaya 139
Jobo 138
Jokhang *(Jo k'on)* 79, 142
Jonang *(Jo naṅ)* 119, 183, *184*

Kadampa *(bKa' gdams pa)* 116
Kafirs 56
Kailāsa, Mt 40, 55, *27*
Kampadsong *(sGam pa rdsoṅ)* 76, *55*
Kanzam pass 55
Karchung *(sKar c'uṅ)* 64, 80
Kashmir (i) 15, 58, 79, 80, 92–4, 117–9, 138–43, 177–83, *127, 146, 156, 164, 208*
Kathmandu 180
Katse *(sKa ts'al)* 78
ke ke ru 55
Keru 78
Khache Penchen *(K'a c'e Paṅ c'en,* Sākyaśri) 178
Khading *(mk'a ldiṅ)* 36
Khalatse *(K'a la rtse?)* 54
Khangsar *(K'aṅ gsar)* 86
Khardsong *(mK'ar rdsoṅ)* 91
Khasarpana 138, 196
Khatangenga *(bKa' t'aṅ sde lṅa)* 140
Khonsher *(K'on bzer)* 61
Khotan(ese) 90, 94, 140–1, 144, 182
Khubilai 136
khyung (k'uṅ) 36, *11*
Khyunglung *(K'yuṅ luṅ)* 40, 49, 57, *58*
Kojarnāth 143, *147*
Kokonor 52, 58
Kongkardsong *(Gon dkar rdsoṅ) 152*
kubum 193–4
Kulu 79, 94, 144
Kungasangpo *(Kun dga' bzaṅ po)* 183

Kun Lun 40
Kunrik *(Kun rig)* *120*
Kurkihar 177
Kurukullā *153*
kuten (sku rten) 115
Kyichu *(sKyid c'u)*, River 80, *59*

Labrangshar *(Bla braṅ šar)* 49
Ladakh 53–4, 59, 73, 76, 92, 181, 196, *125, 134, 135*
Laghman 56
lalitāsana 117
Langdarma *(Glaṅ dar ma)* 90
Leh *(sLeh)* 53–5, 58
Lemurs 49
Lepchas 49, 58
lha bris 139
lhakhang *(lha k'aṅ)* 57, 76, 91, 95
lhapap (lha babs) 113
Lharjechöchang *(Lha rje c'os byaṅ)* 144
Lhasa 49, 52, 61, 63–4, 75, 78, 80, 90, 138, 142, 196, *109, 112, 178, 199*
lhatho (lha t'o) 56
Lhatse *(Lha rtse)* 40, 119, 143, *29, 32, 34, 101, 137, 204*
Lhoṭak *49*
li lugs 94
Lin I-ssu 178
Lo *(Blo*, Mustang) 49, 50, 56, *40*
Lokapālas 15, 194
Lokeśvara 117, *103, 106*
lotsāva 91–2, 119, 137–8
lugs 94
Luk 33, 40, 141, 143, *50, 144, 155, 208*
Luristan *8*

Macdonald, Mrs A.W. 25
Mahāyāna 117
Mahmud of Ghazni 180
Maitreya 119, 138
Maitreya Chökorma 138
Maldo *(Mal gro)* 78
Manasarovar, Lake 51, *4, 6, 7, 24, 25, 31, 39*
maṇḍala 96, 115, 119, *170*
Mangnang *(Maṅ naṅ)* 91, 93, 142, 180–1, *61, 82, 113, 128, 198*
Mañjughosa 93
Mañjuśrī 117, 138, *101*
Mārīcī *143, 205*
Marpa 75–6, *49*
Marpori *(dMar po ri)* 74, 196
Mati 93, *70*
mc'od pai lha mo 115–117
Mesopotamia 37
Miang *(Ma yaṅ?)* 1, *11*
mig 40
Mikyödorje *(Mi bskyod rdo rje)* 138
Milam *(rMi lam?)* *82*
Milarepa 49, 75, *49*
Minusinsk 39
mk'ar 73
mK'yen brtse 62, 137
Moghul 181
Mongol(s) 15, 39, 75, 90, 143, 193
Mongolia 37, 52
Museum of Oriental Art, Rome *202–210*
Muṭhitsenpo *(Mu k'ri brtsan po)* 90
Mu tsung 64
Myaṅ c'uṅ 144

Nachukha *(Nag c'u k'a)* 55
Nalanda 139, 143, 177
Nanam Dorjewangchuk *(sNa nam rDo rje dbaṅ p'yug)* 90
Nanglön *(Naṅ blon)* 62
Nangparnangse *(rNam par snaṅ mdsad) 202*
Nanying *(gNas rñiṅ)* 178, *141*
Narthang *(sNar t'aṅ)* 119, 178, 180, 184, 194, *83, 140, 169, 176, 181, 190–191, 202*
Nebesky-Wojkowitz, R. de 58
Neolithic 33, 57
Nepal(ese) 15, 33, 49, 55, 77–9, 94–5, 113, 119, 138–41, 143, 177–80, 182–4, 194–5, 200, *148, 149, 181, 202–207, 210*
Nesar *(gNas gsar)* 91, 93–4, 144, 182, *60, 159, 162*
Nestorian 39, *11, 29, 112*
Ngariṭatsang *(mNa' ris grwa ts'aṅ)* 116, *87, 88*
Ngarpathang *(Nar pa t'aṅ)* 63
Ngor *(Ṅor)* 183–4, *166, 203, 210*
Norbukhyungtse *(Nor bu k'yuṅ rtse) 197*
Nü *51*
Nubra 40
Nyanṭaksangpopel *(sNan grags bzaṅ do dpal)* 119
Nyelam *(Ñe lam)* 33
Nyen *(gÑan)* 137
Nyethang 178, *172, 175, 178*

Ordos 39
Otantapuri (Paharpur) 90

Padmapāṇi 93–4, 117, 179, *141, 145, 146, 160, 166, 176*
Padmasaṃbhava 74, 196
Padmavajra 138
Pal 178
Pāla 177, 179, *143, 151–153, 157, 158*
Palaeolithic 50
Pangongtsho, Lake *(sPan gon mts'o)* 51
Panjora, Pancora 94
Pan tso ra 93

237

Paolönchen *(dpa' bo Blon c'en)* 178
Parojaya 139
paṭa 177
Peldenlhamo *(dPal ldan lha mo)* 182
Pelkye *(dPal rgyas?)* 57
Pemakarpo *(Pas ma dkar po)* 141
Penam *(sPa nam* or *snam)* 76, *52*
Pendzhikent 181, 183
Phagmotupa *(P'ag mo gru pa)* 75
Phakpa *(aPags pa)* 138
phaong *(p'a boṅ)* 51
Phaongkha *(P'a boṅ k'a)* 74, 196
Phüntshokling *(P'un ts'ogs gliṅ)* 15, 139, 194, *192–196*
Pökhang *(sPos k'aṅ)* 178–9, *160, 165*
Pontic 35
Potala 79, 138
pradakṣiṇa 61
Prajñāpāramitā 115–7, 181, *93, 94, 96, 148, 149*
Prakrit 116
prāṇapratiṣṭhā 116
Preta 49
Pretapuri 49
Pu *(sPu)* 50–1, 56–7
Putön *(Buston)* 138, 193

Qyzil 182–3

Ramoche *(Ra mo c'e)* 77–9, 89
rangchung (raṅ byuṅ) 138
Rapgyeling *(Rab rgyas gliṅ)* 77
Raptenkunsangphakpa *(Rab brtan Kun bzaṅ ap' ags pa)* 119
Rechungphuk *(Ras c'uṅ p'ug)* 49

Recikma *(Ral gcig ma)* 205
Repachen *(Ral pa can)* 75, 80, 195, *47, 178*
Reting *(Rva sgreṅ)* 51
rgyal ba rigs lṅa 195
rgyal sras 144
rgya lugs 94
rgya p'ugs 73, 76
Richardson, H.E. 55, 61, 90, 177, 195, *44, 49, 177–179*
Rigpelhamo *(Rig pai lha mo)* 204
rigs gsum mgon po 195
ri mo 139
Rincana Bhoṭṭa 181
Rinchensangpo *(Rin c'en bzaṅ po)* 80, 90–3, 142, *65, 70, 84, 128*
ringyen (riṅ gyan) 179
Ripumalla 79, 80
Roerich, G. de 51–2, 54–6
Ruben, W. 35
Rudenko, S.I. 39, 63
rva, ra 64
Sachen *(Sa c'en)* 49
sādhu 92
Saga 52, 56
Sakya *(Sa skya)* 49, 51, 95, 116, 137–8, 184, *12, 28, 33, 71, 98–100, 111, 143, 151, 157, 153, 158, 167, 170, 173, 180, 207*
Sakyapa *(Sa skya pa)* 15, 75–6, 119, 177, 184, 193, *203*
Sakyapenchen *(Sa skya Paṇ c'en)* 138
Sākyaśrī 119, 144, 178
Samada 91, 93, 142, 144, *64, 70, 74, 126, 171*
Sāmkāśya 113
Samrava 207
Samye *(bSam yas)* 64, 74–6, 89, 90, 138, 142, 178, 195, *43, 63, 85*
Sanchi 113
Sanghyeghyatsho *(Saṅs rgyas rgya mts'o)* 79

Sanskrit 113–4, 117–8, 177
Sassanid 94, 144, 177
sBa bzhed 195
Sekhang *(gsas k'aṅ)* 57
Sekharguthok *(Sras mk'ar dgu t'og)* 75, *49*
Seligman, G.G. 40
sems 114
Sena 177, 179
Seṅ ge rnam rgyal 76
sgo 114
sgo maṅ 114, 119
Shapgeding *(Sab dge sdiṅs)* 51, 55–6
Shemar *(gSed dmar)* *192–196*
Sherapchungne *(Ser rab abyun gnas)* 138
Sherapgyelthsenpelsangpo *(Ses rab rgyal mts'an dpal bzaṅ po)* 119
Shigatse 119, *13, 19–21, 26, 42*
Siberia 37, 63
siddhas 209
Sikkim(ese) 49, 78
Sinpori *(Srin po ri)* 80
Sirkap 76
Śiva 38
sku mk'an 93
sku mk'ar 73
Snellgrove, D. 177
Sonamṭashi *(bSod nams bkra sis)* 119
Songtsengampo *(Sroṅ btsan sgam po)* 61–3, 74, 77–9, 138, 195–6, *44, 47*
Spiti 55, 58, 144, *129*
Stein, Sir A. 116
stūpa 96, 113–7, 184, *82, 97, 181*
Sumpakhenpo *(Sum pa mk'an po)* 139
Sung 178
sungten (gsuṅ rten) 115
Svayambhūnāth 184, *181*

238

Swat 50, 53-4, 57, 79, 117-8, 196
Syāmā Tārā *205*

Tabo 93, 143, *129, 142*
Tai Erh-chien, Mrs 33
Takmar *(ạBrag dmar)* 74
Tanak *(rTa nag)* 141
T'ang 78, 142, 195, *87*
Tantras, Tantric 113, 118, 193, 199
Tārā 117, 178-9, 190, *105, 175, 205*
Tāranātha 119, 139, 194
Ṭashigang *(bKra šis sgaṅ)* 53
ṭashitagye (bkra šis trags brgyad) 38
Tathāgata 115
Taxila 76
ten (rten) 114-5
Thailand 117
thangka (t'aṅ ka) 142, 177, 181, 183-4, 200, *202-210*
Thangton *(T'aṅ ston)* 119, 59
Ṭhanṭuk *(K'ra ạbrug)* 78, 142, 195, *76, 110*
Ṭhidesongtsen *(K'ri lde sroṅ brtsan)* 62-4, 74, *43, 46*
Ṭhisongdetsen *(K'ri sroṅ lde brtsan)* 49, 74, 78, 80, 89, 141
Ṭhitsukdetsen *(K'ri gtsug lde brtsan)* 64, 140, 195
thoding (mt'o ldiṅ) 34
thokde (t'og rdeu) 34
Tholing *(mT'o gliṅ)* 77, 89, 90, 93, 117, 142-3, 178, 181, *3, 65, 68, 84, 89, 92, 97, 104, 107, 127, 130-132, 136, 164*
Ṭhophu *(K'ro p'u)* 119
thukdam (t'ugs dam) 93
thukten (t'ugs rten) 114-5
Ṭhulnang *(ạP'rul snaṅ)* 77-8, 138

Thumi Lhunṭuptashi *(T'u mi Lhun grub bkra sis)* 119
Tiak *(gTi yag?)* 80, *69*
Tibetan Painted Scrolls 13
Tīrthapuri 49
Tripura 179
Tsang *(gTsaṅ)* 37, 58, 59, 91, 93, 94, 117, 119, *34, 38, 42, 52, 60, 64, 70, 78, 80, 83, 94, 101-103, 126, 159, 160*
Tsangpo *(gTsaṅ po*, Brahmaputra*)* 64, 80, 91, 94, 144, *44, 48*
Tsaparang 40, 49, 73, 93, 142-3, 178, *2, 17, 18, 56, 91, 105, 133, 138, 146, 156*
ts'a ts'as 114-8, *98-108*
Tshepame *(Ts'e dpag med)* 124
Tshogyeltagmar *(mTs'o rgyal Brag dmar)* 49
Tshulṭhimchungne *(Ts'ul k'rims ạbyuṅ gnas)* 138
Tshurphu *(mTs'ur p'u)* 64
Tsongkhapa 193
Tsuglagkhang 64, 79
t'ugs 114
Tukcha 49
Tumchuq 182
Tun huang 38, 55, 57
Turfan 182
Tuṣita 113

Uḍḍiyana 196
Ushangdo *(U saṅ rdo* or *On caṅ rdo)* 74, 80, *66, 67*
Ushkur 80
Üssukhar *(dBus su mk'ar)* 91
ütok (dbu t'og) 79
Uyghur(s) 116, 141

Vairocana *202*
Vaiśravaṇa 194
Vajrabhairava *206*
Vajradharma *120, 152*

Vajrāpaṇi 93, 143, *118, 210*
varadamudrā 205
Vibhūticandra 80
Vijaya 139
Vikramaśīlā 89
Viśvakarman 138
vitarka-mudrā 202

Waddell, L.A. 40
Wylie 75

yab yum 179
Yamalung *(gYa' ma luṅ)* 74
Yamunā 143, *137*
Yandogtsho *(Yar ạbrog mts'o)* 40, *36, 41*
Yarlung *(Yar kluṅs)* 40, 49, 61, 63, 73-5, *5, 10, 37*
Yemar *(gYe dmar)* 144
Yerpa 49, 142
Yüan 15, 38-9, 184, 193, *11, 29, 72, 73, 111, 180*
Yüeh-chi 35
Yumbulhakhar *(Yum bu lha mk'ar)* 73, 76, *48*

Zhailhakhang *(Žva'i lha k'aṅ)* 64
Zhalu *(Ža lu)* 138, 193, *72, 73, 103, 201*
Zhidekar *(gŽi dse mk'ar?)* 51
Zhithok *(bŽi t'og)* 177
Zhönnuö *(gŽon nu 'od)* 93
zigs 40
Zinchi *(rDsiṅ p'yi)* 161
Ziöbarva *(gZi 'od ạbar ba)* 138
zla ñi 113
zoba (bzo ba) 139
žol rdo riṅ 196
Zurkhar *(Zur mk'ar* or *Zuṅ mk'ar)* 74

239

FINISHED IN AUGUST 1973

THE TEXT AND ILLUSTRATIONS IN THIS VOLUME
WERE PRINTED ON THE PRESS OF
NAGEL PUBLISHERS IN GENEVA

BINDING BY NAGEL PUBLISHERS IN GENEVA

OFFSET COLOUR SEPARATIONS BY
GRAVOR SA IN BIENNE

LEGAL DEPOSIT No 575

PRINTED IN SWITZERLAND